The
Royal
Blue & Gold
Cook Book

The Royal Blue & Gold Cook Book

by The Marchioness of Cambridge

Jupiter Books London

Acknowledgements

The Marchioness of Cambridge
wishes to acknowledge
My Granddaughter Miss Sarah Whitley
Miss Dorothy Croasdale
Miss Muriel Sandiforth
without whose help this book could not have
been possible.

Editor : Judith Schecter
Design : Roger Hyde
Illustration : Janet Mitchener

For consultation we gratefully acknowledge
the help of:
Mr. R. E. Sellens, Head Chef, Fortnum & Mason
Mr. Arthur Lunn, Fortnum & Mason

All photographs reproduced with the kind
permission of Syndication International.

ISBN 0 904041 03 4
Copyright 1974 by Jupiter Books (London) Ltd.

Printed and bound in Spain by
Roner S.A., Madrid
Dep. legal S.S. 484 -74

CONTENTS

The Royal British Legion Women's Section

This Organisation of women was founded in 1921 shortly after the Royal British Legion came into being.

Its aim is to promote the welfare and safeguard the interests of the widows, children and dependants of those who have served in the Forces of the Crown and also of ex-servicewomen. It also exists to augment the welfare work of the Royal British Legion and to assist them with the Earl Haig Fund (Poppy Appeal), although the Section accepts no financial benefit from this appeal.

It is the only body of women organised for this purpose. Through its 3,000 Branches, the Section offers companionship, help and advice to those in need and eligible, and it is responsible for financing and running Welfare Schemes as follows.

Widow's Allowances

This Scheme started in 1938 for the purpose of granting a small weekly allowance to a limited number of widows of ex-servicemen suffering very real hardship. Those eligible must be in need and unable to work on account of age, health or other special cause and must have applied for Social Security Benefits or other State assistance before an application can be considered.

Rest Homes

The Women's Section runs two Rest Homes free of charge. They are available to the wives and widows of ex-servicemen, and ex-servicewomen who are in need of rest on medical advice.

Flatlets

This latest venture started in 1964 with the conversion of three houses into flatlets, in London, Southport and Belfast. In addition in 1971 a purpose-built block of flatlets was officially opened by Her Majesty Queen Elizabeth The Queen Mother in Haslemere, Surrey. These flatlets provide unfurnished accommodation for 60 needy widows of ex-servicemen and some ex-servicewomen.

Welfare Fund

A general Welfare fund is available for any special work of the Women's Section not covered by the foregoing. All these welfare Schemes have been inaugurated, and are maintained, solely by voluntary donations from the Women's Section Branches in this Country.

Women's Section Branches undertake to visit Hospital patients and elderly war widows in their homes. They sell goods made by disabled ex-servicemen and women as well as serving on War Pensions and other Welfare Committees.

INTRODUCTION

My interest in cooking began at the age of 16 when I joined the Red Cross hoping to do some nursing. However, they took one look at me and sent me to work in the kitchens at Hampton Court. For four months I helped cook the most indescribably nasty food. After being sacked for checking the cook when we were cooking what was supposed to be beef, but was actually horse, I went up to Appleby to the Red House Hospital, where I remained until the end of the war. I will always remember with affection the people of Appleby who turned me into a reasonably good cook.

The old cook in my first job had a true novice on her hands when I was made second cook. One day, she was to be off duty. She led me to the larder where there were three whole carcasses of sheep hanging up, and pronounced that I was to cut them up into joints for lunch the following day. I did not even know how to boil an egg at that time! Undaunted, I assured her it would be finished in time. I then found an orderly and asked him if there was a butcher amongst the patients. In 10 minutes, he was back with a charming young man who was delighted to spend an afternoon at his civilian job, and all it cost me was a packet of cigarettes.

When I married and went to London, we entertained on a large scale, and I was lucky to have an excellent cook who enjoyed planning with me the menus for our dinner parties. On one occasion, the French Ambassador paid me the gracious compliment that the average dinner in England was excellent, though usually too lavish, but mine was perfect.

During the evacuation from Dunkirk, I received a telephone call from a friend asking if I could spare my cook to help at the feeding centre at Euston Station. My cook was out, so I decided to go along myself. From 5 o'clock until midnight, my friend and I cooked 60 dozen eggs with bacon and sausages. That was an experience I will always remember.

Now that my cook is semi-retired, I quite enjoy doing much of my own cooking. I am rather lazy and have one or two easy dishes I have invented. It is really important to be able to cook a good meal at a moment's notice, but it is also essential to be adventurous.

I think perhaps my inventive mind went a little too far during the war. Having been presented with a fine piece of fresh salmon, I found I had no olive oil with which to make the mayonnaise. Four people enjoyed cold mayonnaise of salmon for lunch, and as far as I know, suffered no ill effects. The sauce was made with liquid paraffin—and they all had a second helping!

For both the adventurous and timid cooks, I hope these recipes will provide as much pleasurable dining as they have for me.

DOROTHY CAMBRIDGE

METRIC CONVERSION TABLE

Avoirdupois	Metric *(suggested conversion to nearest unit of 25)*
1 ounce	25 grams
8 ounces	225 grams
12 ounces	350 grams
16 ounces	450 grams

Liquid Measures

$\frac{1}{4}$ pint	150 millilitres
$\frac{1}{2}$ pint	275 millilitres
$\frac{3}{4}$ pint	425 millilitres
1 pint	575 millilitres

Hors d'Oeuvres and Savouries

Anglesey Hare Pâté The Marquess of Anglesey

Ham Sticks Sonja Henie

Provence Flan The Marchioness of Cambridge

Dutch Croûtons The Lady Maud Carnegie

Curried Cheese Mrs. Laurence Carr

Kisch au Parmesan H.R.H. Princess Alice, Countess of Athlone

Cold Cheese Creams The Lady Maud Carnegie

Fried Fresh Herrings with Mustard Sauce Their Majesties
King George VI and Queen Elizabeth

Anchovy Fritters Mrs. Laurence Carr

Kipper Savoury The Marchioness of Cambridge

Éperlans L' Aurore Mrs. Butler-Brooke

Lobster Cocktails The Marchioness of Cambridge

Amandes à la Diable Mrs. Andrews, Cook to
Mrs. Oliver Martin-Smith

Berkeley Sandwich H.R.H. The Duchess of Gloucester

Banana Savoury Mrs. Laurence Carr

Anglesey Hare Pâté

Ingredients

young hare
2 carrots
2 stalks celery
1 onion, chopped
bouquet garni of parsley, thyme, bay leaf, and winter savory
1 leek, if desired
1-2 cloves garlic
$\frac{1}{4}$ cup veal or beef stock
$\frac{1}{3}$-$\frac{1}{2}$ cup port
4 tablespoons butter, melted

Preparation

Have the hare trimmed and cut into joints. Place in a large stewing pan with the vegetables. The bouquet garni should be secured in a piece of muslin. More parsley can be added to the pot along with the other vegetables. Crush 1–2 cloves of garlic, distributing the garlic and vegetables among the pieces of meat. Cover with cold water. Bring to a boil, skim the surface and simmer gently for six hours.

Remove the meat from the bone. Mince and add more pressed garlic if desired. Fold in some of the stock from the hare. If the seasoning needs to be corrected, add a few tablespoons of stock on hand. Stir in port. Return mixture to the heat, in a saucepan and stir until the mixture is well blended. The pâté should now be of a good consistency, but not too thick.

Pour the pâté into a terrine and allow to cool. When it is quite cold, seal with the butter. The seal helps retain the flavour and freshness of the pâté.

The Marquess of Anglesey

Ham Sticks

Ingredients to serve 4
**12 thin Italian bread
sticks
6 thin slices
prosciutto or
Parma ham
Dijon mustard
oil**

Preparation
Select paper-thin slices of spicy ham;
Prosciutto or Parma are a complement to
the mustard and bake well. The slices
should be five to six inches across, and
trimmed of fat. Cut the slices in half.
Spread a thin layer of Dijon-type mustard or horseradish mustard on each of
the 12 ham slices.

Wrap the paper-thin slices around the
bread sticks, allowing a bit of bread stick
to show from either end. Brush the outside with vegetable oil or shortening.
Bake at a moderate oven until golden
brown, about 7–8 minutes.

Serve piping hot with assorted olives,
pickles, and crudités.

Sonja Henie

Provence Flan

Ingredients to serve 6
Flan case:
8 oz. plain flour
½ teaspoon salt
4 oz. butter
1 egg
3 tablespoons cold
    water
Filling:
6-10 onions, depend-
    ing upon size
  1 tablespoon butter
    or margarine
  ½ teaspoon brown
    sugar
    small tin
    anchovies
    chopped
    pimiento and
    parsley,
    optional

Preparation

Prepare the flan case first, so that it has time to cool before filling. The addition of an egg to this pastry increases its richness and flavour. Sift the flour into a large cold bowl. Make a well in the centre and add the salt, butter, and water. The butter should be pre-cut into small bits for quick blending. Work the liquid mixture with fingertips, blending the flour gradually. Knead lightly, on a floured board, being careful not to overwork the dough. Loosely wrap and allow it to rest in the refrigerator for an hour. Bake in fairly hot oven (400°F, Mark 6) for 15 minutes. Allow flan case to cool before filling.

Slice onions either across or in strips. Cover with cold water and bring to a boil. Blanch onions for 2 minutes and transfer to large frying pan. Add butter and brown sugar, tossing mixture lightly over medium heat until the onions are soft and a golden glazed colour. Cool; then fill baked flan case. Decorate with trellis work of anchovies, dotted with pimiento.

Alternatively, onion layers may be accented with pimientoes and parsley, chopped for colour, topping the flan with browned breadcrumbs.

The Marchioness of Cambridge

12

Dutch Croûtons

Ingredients
  4 oz. sharp cheese
1½ oz. butter
  2 hard-boiled eggs
  6 croûtons fried
     bread
     parsley
     paprika

Preparation
Allow the cheese to reach room temperature. This precaution ensures the cheese will blend and spread properly. Separate the hard-boiled yolks from whites. Chop whites and reserve for garnish. Grate the cheese, setting aside 1 tbsp. for garnish. Pound cheese and egg yolks together in a mortar. Add softened butter until it is of spreading consistency. Lightly season with paprika.

Spread this mixture thickly on the fried bread croûtons, using a broad butter spatula. Brown slowly under the grill, about 8–10 minutes. Sprinkle some reserved grated cheese and the chopped whites of the eggs over the tops.

Garnish with parsley and serve on a pre-heated platter.

The Lady Maud Carnegie

Curried Cheese

Ingredients to serve 4
- **2 oz. Cheddar cheese, grated**
- **$\frac{1}{3}$ pint cream**
- **$1\frac{1}{2}$ oz. flour**
- **$1\frac{1}{2}$ oz. butter**
- **2 eggs, beaten generous pinch curry powder**
- **1 egg, beaten olive oil, or vegetable oil, if preferred**

Preparation

In a medium sized, high-sided saucepan, slowly melt grated cheese over medium heat, stirring the cream into the mixture. The sauce base will not stick if it is stirred constantly. However, if you are at all hesitant about maintaining the proper temperature, set the saucepan in a bain marie. This method takes slightly more time, but ensures that the mixture won't stick to the pan.

Gradually add flour, then the butter, cut into small bits. When blended, carefully add the two beaten eggs and the curry powder, being sure to whisk the mixture constantly. Continue stirring until the mixture is thick enough to coat a wooden spoon. Turn into one-inch deep pan, preferably square and small. Refrigerate.

When the mixture is cold completely through, cut into squares. Dip first into seasoned beaten egg, then breadcrumbs and fry in hot olive oil until golden brown. Serve with plain water biscuits.

Mrs. Laurence Carr

Kisch au Parmesan

Ingredients
3 oz. Parmesan
cheese
½ pint milk
3 egg yolks
⅛ pint cream
salt
cayenne pepper

Preparation
Slice the Parmesan cheese so that it will melt gradually and evenly. Bring ½ pint milk to a slow boil. Add the cheese and allow to cook at just below the boiling point for half an hour.

If preferred, the mixture may be cooked over a bain marie to ensure the liquid does not stick nor evaporate too much. Strain this mixture through muslin.

Gently whisk three egg yolks in medium-sized bowl. Continue to whisk the yolks while adding the cream.

Slowly stir in the strained milk mixture, making a liquid custard. Season to taste with salt. Pour the mixture into individual ramekins and sprinkle cayenne pepper lightly over the top. Steam for half an hour, either in a steamer on the burner, or in a large pan filled halfway with water, set in a moderately hot oven (375° or Mark 5).

The custard should not be very stiff.

H.R.H. Princess Alice,
Countess of Athlone

Cold Cheese Creams

Ingredients to serve 6
1-2 sheets gelatine
5 oz. aspic jelly
½ tsp mustard,
to taste
¼ pt. cream
1½ oz. Parmesan
cheese
1½ oz. Roquefort
cheese
salt
cayenne pepper
chopped parsley

Preparation

Melt gelatine in a tablespoonful of water. Melt the aspic jelly just enough to allow it to blend with the gelatine. Strain gelatine into the aspic. Mix a small amount of mustard with a tablespoonful of the aspic jelly. The amount of mustard used depends on the variety; a Dijon-type is best. Add the mustard and aspic to the remainder of the aspic jelly. Whip vigorously until frothy.

Whisk the cream until fairly stiff. Stir grated Roquefort and Parmesan cheese into the cream with a gentle folding motion. Fold in the whipped aspic, carefully blending all ingredients.

Season with salt and cayenne pepper. Turn into individual ramekins or soufflé cases. To keep a neat "collar" around the top of each mould, fasten a band of greaseproof paper around the case, as for a soufflé.

For the best results, put on ice to set. Sprinkle with parsley just before serving.

The Lady Maud Carnegie

Fried Fresh Herrings with Mustard Sauce

Ingredients to serve 6
**6-10 fresh herrings,
    depending upon
    size
5 tablespoons flour
1 egg, beaten
    seasoned
        breadcrumbs
        vegetable oil or
        shortening**
Mustard sauce
  **2 tablespoons butter
  2 tablespoons
    chopped onions
  2 tablespoons flour
  1 pint hot milk
  $\frac{1}{2}$ teaspoon salt
  $\frac{1}{4}$ teaspoon white
    pepper
  pinch freshly
    grated nutmeg
1-2 teaspoons
    prepared Dijon
    mustard
  $\frac{1}{2}$ teaspoon vinegar
  salt and pepper**

Preparation
Split open the herrings, removing the roe and the bone. Wash and dry thoroughly. Lightly flour the fillets, then dip them individually, first into the beaten egg, then into the seasoned breadcrumbs. Fry each fillet in sizzling oil or shortening, keeping the fat at an even, high temperature. As each fillet turns a golden brown, remove to a heated tray.

The mustard sauce requires a simple Béchamel sauce as its base. Melt the butter in a small, heavy saucepan. Add the onions as soon as the butter is melted, and cook over medium heat for 3 minutes. Blend in flour. Slowly stir in milk, stirring constantly until smooth. Add salt, pepper, and nutmeg, stirring constantly over low heat for 15 minutes, or allow to rest, covered, near the heat to make a thorough infusion.

Mix a small amount of vinegar with the mustard, tasting to see that the vinegar does not overpower the mustard flavour. Add the mustard gradually to the Béchamel sauce, tasting as you blend. Add salt and pepper to taste.

Serve either in separate sauceboat, or decoratively sauced over the fillets.

**Their Majesties King George VI
and Queen Elizabeth**

Anchovy Fritters

Ingredients

2 hard-boiled egg
  yolks
6 anchovy fillets
1 teaspoon capers
2 oz. butter
1 tablespoon parsley
1 oz. grated Parmesan
  cheese
1 raw egg yolk
  salt, paprika,
  pepper
1 tablespoon seasoned
  breadcrumbs
  vegetable oil or
  shortening

Preparation

Pound the yolks in a mortar with the cut-up anchovy fillets. Mix in the capers, softened butter and parsley until the mixture is thoroughly blended. Add the grated Parmesan cheese.

Rub the mixture through a fine sieve, twice if necessary. Add the raw egg yolk and 1 tablespoon breadcrumbs. Season with pepper, paprika, and salt to taste.

Form the mixture into small rounds, the size of hors d'oeuvre meatballs. The consistency should be that of a paste. Roll each round in breadcrumbs, then in beaten egg, then in breadcrumbs for a final coating. Drop into hot fat and fry until golden brown. The rounds will retain their shape if they are completely coated, and the fat is bubbling hot.

Mrs. Laurence Carr

Kipper Savoury

Ingredients to serve 4
**2 packages kipper
fillets**
½ pint double cream
salt
pepper
toast croûtons

Preparation
A quick delicious savoury for unexpected guests can be made with little effort and a well-stocked refrigerator. Boil two packages of boneless kipper fillets in water, in the bag, according to the instructions on the package.

Remove kipper fillets and separate them, draining on kitchen towelling if necessary. Place them in a flat serving dish. Pour double cream over fillets to masque them completely. Season with salt and freshly ground pepper.

Bake in moderately hot oven (375°F, mark 5) for 12 minutes.

Arrange toast triangles on platter with the kipper fillets. Or serve toast separately.

The Marchioness of Cambridge

Éperlans L'Aurore

Ingredients
1 small whiting
1 egg
$\frac{1}{4}$ pint cream
salt
freshly ground
pepper
6 smelts
2 tablespoons butter,
melted
breadcrumbs
Hollandaise sauce
juice of $\frac{1}{2}$ lemon
1 teaspoon water
2 egg yolks
4 oz. butter
salt
cayenne pepper

Preparation
Pound the whiting in a mortar. Mix with one egg, $\frac{1}{4}$ pint cream. Add freshly ground pepper from the mill, and salt to taste.

Bone 6 smelts along the back. Clean and wipe completely dry. Stuff with the above forcemeat using a cocktail fork or similar implement. Close fish so that no forcemeat protrudes from the sides. Toothpicks may be inserted to ensure the smelts retain their shape.

Dip in melted butter, then in the breadcrumbs. Grill until golden brown. Serve with the following Hollandaise sauce: Put a small bowl over a saucepan of simmering water. Put water and lemon juice in bowl, adding the egg yolks, one at a time. Add $\frac{1}{2}$ oz. butter in very small bits, whisking thoroughly until stiff. Remove the saucepan from the heat, and add the remaining butter in small pieces, whisking constantly. Season with salt and cayenne pepper.

Mrs. Butler-Brooke

Lobster Cocktails

Ingredients to serve 6
1 **medium lobster**
  cos or bib lettuce
4 **tablespoons**
  mayonnaise
1 **tablespoon**
  Worcester sauce
1 **tablespoon tomato**
  ketchup
1 **tablespoon double**
  cream
  dash of cayenne
  pepper
  lemon and capers
  to garnish

Preparation
Twist the large claws off the lobster and crack them, being careful not to injure the flesh. Remove the smaller claws. Split the lobster down the middle of the back, from head to tail using a sharp, small knife. Remove the insides and the spongy gills.

Take the meat from the large claws and the back and tail, and cut into small pieces.

Line custard glasses or wide compote cups with the smaller, tender leaves of lettuce. Place the chopped lobster on the lettuce bed. Cover with a sauce made from the remaining five ingredients. This sauce should be allowed to chill after blending for a few hours in the refrigerator.

Decorate with pinwheels of lemon and a few capers.

The Marchioness of Cambridge

Amandes à la Diable

Ingredients to serve 4
2 oz. almonds
3 oz. chopped
  gherkins
1 tablespoon chutney
1 teaspoon Harvey
  sauce
1 teaspoon olive oil
  freshly ground
    pepper
  salt
  dash cayenne
  fried bread
    croûtons

Preparation
Blanch the shelled almonds by dropping them into boiling water and leaving them for a few minutes. Squeeze each one between the thumb and forefinger and the brown skin will slip off quite easily. Rinse in cold water and dry on a cloth.

Shred the nuts and fry lightly in olive oil over medium heat for a few minutes. Allow them to brown just lightly.

Mix the gherkins and chutney with the sauce. Add the seasoning. Stir in the fried almonds and heat for five minutes in a saucepan. Mound on freshly toasted croûtons and serve piping hot.

Mrs. Andrews,
Cook to Mrs. Oliver Martin-Smith

Berkeley Sandwich

Ingredients to serve 4
**3 oz. Cheddar
cheese
3 anchovies
2 hard-boiled eggs
pinch fresh
tarragon and
chervil
1-2 tablespoons butter
cos lettuce
brown bread,
sliced very thinly**

Preparation
Pound the Cheddar cheese with the anchovies until well blended. Separate the hard-boiled egg yolks from the whites. Add the yolks with the herbs, preferably the snipped, fresh variety. Pass the mixture through a sieve.

Mix in a teaspoon of butter, which has been allowed to soften, and cream with a wooden spoon.

Add more butter as needed to form a paste.

Spread on thin slices of brown bread. Lay a small leaf of cos lettuce on each slice spread with paste. Stack the slices four deep and trim the lettuce neatly round the edges, finishing with a plain slice of buttered brown bread.

Press the sandwiches firmly for a few hours. Cut into finger sandwiches of assorted shapes.

H.R.H. The Duchess of Gloucester

Banana Savoury

Ingredients to serve 4
2 bananas
½ oz. butter
1 teaspoon curry powder
1 teaspoon chutney
salt
cayenne pepper
1 tablespoon biscuit crumbs
1 tablespoon white wine or stock
croûtons of fried bread
salted almonds

Preparation
Cut the bananas into dice. Heat the butter over medium heat, not letting it brown. Add the banana, chutney, curry powder and seasonings. Cook for 2–3 minutes, only stirring occasionally. If the dish is mixed too well, the result will be an unappetising mixture.

Add the biscuit crumbs and wine or stock, if preferred. Cook a few minutes longer.

Toast the croûtons just before serving so that they are quite crisp and hot. Spread the mixture on the croûtons and decorate with salted, toasted almonds in slivers.

Mrs. Laurence Carr

Soups

Borscht à la Russe The Berkeley Hotel, London
Crab Soup Lady Dynoven
Onion Soup Mrs. Ian Erskine
Clear Tomato Soup Mrs. Andrews, Cook to
Mrs. Oliver Martin-Smith
Lobster Soup The Lady Maud Carnegie

Borscht à la Russe

Ingredients to serve 4
- **3 raw beetroot**
- **2 leeks**
- **½ small white cabbage**
- **2 small stalks celery**
- **2 teaspoons butter**
- **1-2 pints duck or beef broth**
- **3 tablespoons beetroot juice**
- **1 pound brisket or shin beef**
- **small duck**
- **2 Frankfurter sausages**
- **Sour cream**

Preparation

Cut the beetroot into fine julienne strips. Slice the leeks and cabbage. Leave the light green leaves on the celery stalks and split lengthwise. Heat the vegetables in butter, for five minutes.

Add the broth; the flavour will be improved by the use of duck broth, but plain broth may be substituted. Stir in the beetroot juice; add the beef and the duck, cut into quarters. The broth should simmer, and never reach the boiling point.

Skim the surface at least three times. Simmer for 2 to 3 hours, until the meat is tender.

Remove the meat. Cut the beef into small slices and return to the soup. Boil two Frankfurter sausages and slice into the soup.

Remove the meat from the breast of the duck. Shred, and use as garnish for the soup.

Serve in soup tureen either with dollops of sour cream on the top, or sour cream passed separately.

The Berkeley Hotel, London

Crab Soup

Ingredients
1 pint milk
1 pound crab meat
juice of one onion
$\frac{1}{2}$ pint cream
1 tablespoon "Maggi" flavouring
2 oz. butter
2 tablespoons flour
salt
pepper
$\frac{1}{4}$ cup chicken stock
2 tablespoons sherry

Preparation
In the top of a double saucepan put the milk and the crab meat, gently flaked. Add the juice of one onion which can be squeezed through a piece of muslin. Boil gently over water for 20 minutes.

Add $\frac{1}{2}$ pint cream, the flavouring and the butter which has been blended with the flour. If the butter is softened before blending with the flour, the mixture will not become lumpy. Keep the soup just under the boiling point for another 15 minutes.

Strain the liquid into another pan. Return to low heat. Add salt, pepper and only enough chicken stock to taste; correct the seasoning, adding more chicken stock if necessary.

Add sherry to taste. Serve in tureen, garnished with parsley or watercress.

Lady Dynoven

Onion Soup

Ingredients to serve 4
5 medium-sized onions
2 oz. butter
2 oz. light vegetable oil
3 cups beef broth
6 slices dried French bread
olive oil
salt
pepper
$\frac{1}{4}$ pound grated Gruyère or Parmesan cheese

Preparation
Slice the onions in fine thin slices. Heat the butter and oil together in a large frying pan. Cook the onions in the oil and butter for 45 minutes. They must be well cooked and should never brown. Stir them occasionally to prevent them from browning, and to be sure they are all cooked evenly.

Cover with broth, adding some water if necessary. Cover the pan and cook slowly for one hour.

Just before serving, float the slices of bread, which have been lightly fried in olive oil, on the top of the soup. The croûtons may also be brushed with oil and slowly browned in the oven. Continue boiling for a minute or two.

Serve with grated Gruyère or Parmesan cheese.

Mrs. Ian Erskine

Clear Tomato Soup

Ingredients
1 quart white stock
1 pound tomatoes
bay leaf
8 white peppercorns
(if available) or
black peppercorns
2 egg shells
2 egg whites
pinch of sugar
pinch of salt

Preparation
Start with a good white stock made by simmering 4 oz. veal, 2 oz. veal bones, one onion, quartered, one carrot and salt and peppercorns for 2–3 hours. Or use other homemade stock.

Put the quart of stock in a large saucepan with the tomatoes, sliced. Add the bay leaf, peppercorns and the two egg shells which have been crushed. Whisk the two egg whites just lightly, and add to the stock.

Whisk the soup over the fire until it reaches the boiling point. Set it aside, off the fire, and allow to simmer gently for 10 minutes. Strain through a soup cloth.

Just before serving, add a generous pinch of sugar and salt. Correct seasoning.

Mrs. Andrews,
Cook to Mrs. Oliver Martin-Smith

Lobster Soup

Ingredients to serve 6
**1 large or 2 small
boiled hen lobsters
1½ oz. flour
pinch of pounded
mace
2 quarts water
1 teaspoon anchovy
essence
1 egg
juice of half a
lemon
2 oz. butter
salt
pepper
breadcrumbs**

Preparation
Carefully select the meat from the shells of the lobsters, including the large claws. Pound the shells and the small claws in a mortar, then place both in a stew-pan with the water. Simmer for one hour. Strain the liquor into a bowl. Pound half the spawn with the butter, rolled in a small amount of the flour. Rub this mixture through a sieve into the strained soup. Allow soup to simmer without boiling to retain the colour, about 10 minutes. Add the anchovy essence and the juice of half a lemon.

Make forcemeat balls of the remaining lobster spawn which has been minced and blended with the breadcrumbs, mace, salt and pepper. Moisten with beaten egg. Roll in flour, and drop lightly into the soup to warm through.

Serve either in bowls, or a large tureen, decorated with large prawns or crayfish.

The Lady Maud Carnegie

Eggs

La Quiche de Lorraine Their Majesties
King George VI and Queen Elizabeth
Oeufs à la Davaillier Mrs. Fraser, Cook to Philip Hodgson, Esq.
Omelette with Asparagus Sproue H.R.H. Princess Marina,
Duchess of Kent
Omelette Luigi Luigi's, London
Spanish Omelette The Marchioness of Cambridge
Omelette Mikado The Savoy Hotel, London
Devilled Eggs Mrs. Ian Erskine
Poached Eggs Grand Duo Mrs. Lawson Johnson
Barquettes d'Oeuf Mrs. McGuinness, Cook to Lady Hothfield
Oeufs Piquants Mrs. Fraser, Cook to Philip Hodgson, Esq.
Eggs à la Boston The Lady Wraxell
Soufflé d'Oeufs Claridge's Claridge's, London
Filling for Egg Tartlets The Marchioness of Cambridge
Oeufs Brouillés Hongroise Mrs. Williams
Egg Mousse The Marchioness of Cambridge

La Quiche de Lorraine

Ingredients
½ **pint milk**
¼ **pint cream**
4 **tablespoons grated**
   Emmentaler cheese
6 **egg yolks**
1 **egg**
   cayenne pepper

Preparation
Line a flan ring with short pastry. (See page 12 for shortcrust pastry recipe given for Provence flan.)

Bake the flan case just until cooked partially through. The case should not start to brown, as the final baking will be done with the filling, at a later stage. The flan case should be baked enough, however, to hold a liquid mixture.

Mix the milk and cream and blend in the yolks, one at a time. Add the whole egg and the grated cheese. Mix thoroughly and add the cayenne. Pass through a fine strainer. Pour into prepared flan case and bake in fairly hot oven (400°F, Mark 6) for 20–35 minutes depending on the temperature of your oven. The filling must be firmly set. Serve very hot, straight from the oven.

**Their Majesties, King George VI
and Queen Elizabeth**

Oeufs à la Davaillier

Ingredients to serve 4
6 slices bread
3 tablespoons Bovril
2 tablespoons
  English mustard
  salt and pepper
½ pound grated
  Cheddar cheese
1 pound raw sausage
  meat
6 eggs
3 tablespoons cream

Preparation

Remove the crusts from the bread. Toast very lightly (about one minute). Spread with a very thin layer of Bovril or glaze, if preferred. Spread on this layer a small amount of the mustard seasoned with salt and pepper. Dust with ¼ pound of the grated cheese. Brown quickly in a moderate oven in the dish it will be served in, preferably a large, shallow au gratin dish.

Rub some raw sausage meat through a sieve and spread about ¼ inch thick on the toast. Make a hollow in the centre of each. Carefully fill the depressions with a raw egg. Cover with the following cheese mixture: Combine the remaining ¼ pound Cheddar cheese with three tablespoons cream over low heat. When the cheese cream is melted, pour over the eggs.

Bake in fairly hot oven (400°F, Mark 6) for 7–10 minutes, or until browned.

Mrs. Fraser,
Cook to Philip Hodgson, Esq.

Omelette with Asparagus Sproue

Ingredients to serve 4
1 pound asparagus
5 eggs
  salt
  pepper
1 tablespoon water
2 oz. butter
1 tablespoon cream

Preparation

Cook the asparagus spears in an asparagus cooker or a frying pan, just covered with boiling water. Choose young, tender asparagus for best results. Do not crowd the spears; cook for about 8 minutes, just until tender.

Cut the spears into small pieces and mix with the eggs, beaten with 1 tablespoon water, salt, and pepper. Reserve the tips and keep them warm in a saucepan until the finishing stage of the omelette. Heat the butter, and when sizzling, add the egg and asparagus mixture and cook quickly, lifting the omelette with a wooden spatula or fork to cook thoroughly. Continue cooking until the top is lightly set and the underside is brown. Split the top and carefully set the asparagus tips in the ridge.

Pour the cream along the asparagus tips and either cover to puff omelette slightly, or brown for one minute under the grill.

H.R.H. Princess Marina,
Duchess of Kent

Omelette Luigi

Ingredients to serve 4
- **5 eggs**
- **$2\frac{1}{2}$ tablespoons butter**
- **1 small smoked haddock**
- **1 tablespoon water**
- **salt**
- **pepper**
- **paprika**
- **chervil**
- **3 tablespoons double cream**
- **$\frac{1}{4}$ cup grated Gruyère or Emmentaler cheese**

Preparation

Remove the tail and fins from the smoked haddock. Cut the fish in small pieces and put in small frying pan, covered just barely with the milk. Add some pepper to taste and a small pat ot butter. Simmer gently until tender, about 8–10 minutes. Drain.

Beat the eggs with the water and seasonings. Heat the butter to sizzling and pour in the eggs mixed with the smoked haddock. Stir with fork, keeping the pieces of haddock as whole as possible. Move the cooked mixture to the centre of the pan, allowing the uncooked mixture to come into contact with the pan surfaces.

Fold the omelette in half. Turn out on heated plate and cover with the double cream combined with grated cheese and just heated to a thick, creamy consistency. Quickly brown under the grill, and serve at once.

Luigi's, London

Spanish Omelette

Ingredients to serve 4
5 **eggs**
  salt
  pepper
1 **teaspoon water**
1 **tablespoon butter**
$\frac{1}{4}$ **cup chopped onions**
$\frac{1}{8}$ **cup pimientoes**
$\frac{1}{2}$ **cup thinly sliced**
  potatoes
2 **tablespoons butter**

Preparation
Heat the filling for omelette just before beating the eggs. Make the filling by mixing the chopped onions, pimientoes in small strips, and the thinly sliced potatoes which have been lightly sauteed in 2 tablespoons butter.

Break the eggs into a bowl and season with salt and pepper. Beat the eggs lightly with a fork until the whites and yolks are mixed. Add 1 teaspoon water to the eggs and mix in the warmed filling of vegetables.

Heat the butter in a pan reserved for omelettes and when it is sizzling hot, pour the egg mixture all at once into the pan. It should bubble immediately.

Gently lift the bottom of the omelette and allow the liquid to run to the sides of the pan. When the omelette has cooked through on the underside and is mostly set on top, flip it over with one smooth, quick motion, and cook for another minute.

The Marchioness of Cambridge

Omelette Mikado

Ingredients to serve 4
5 eggs
  salt
  pepper
  dash dill weed
2 teaspoons water
2 teaspoons butter
**4 tablespoons back fin
   crab meat**
  **lobster or shrimp
   sauce**
½ cup Mornay sauce

Preparation
Mix the eggs, salt and pepper with the dill weed. Add the water and cook as with other omelettes in hot butter until almost set.

This omelette is folded in thirds. Before the top surface has cooked completely through, place in the centre third two tablespoons of crab meat which has been mixed with just a teaspoon or two of bottled lobster or shrimp sauce. Now fold into thirds. Put the omelette on a flame-proof serving platter and pour over top ½ cup Mornay sauce. Glaze under the grill for a minute or two.

A simple sauce Mornay can be made by adding one ounce of grated Gruyère or Cheddar, or a combination of both to the basic Béchamel sauce.

The Savoy Hotel, London

Devilled Eggs

Ingredients to serve 4
- **1 tablespoon butter or margarine**
- **1 oz. butter**
- **4 eggs**
- **2 tablespoons milk**
- **salt**
- **cayenne pepper**
- **$1\frac{1}{2}$ teaspoons prepared mustard**
- **1 tablespoon chutney**
- **2 tablespoons capers**
- **2 eggs**

Preparation

Melt the butter or margarine in a frying pan and fry the eggs carefully until the whites are set, but not hard. Meanwhile, melt the 1 oz. butter in a saucepan. Add the milk, salt, and cayenne and bring to a boil.

Add the mustard, chutney, and the two eggs, well beaten. Stir the mixture over a low fire, until the sauce is like thick cream, never allowing it to come to a boil. Add the chopped capers and pour the sauce over the fried eggs. The dish may be warmed slightly under the grill or in a very hot oven for a few minutes, as it must be served very hot.

Mrs. Ian Erskine

Poached Eggs Grand Duo

Ingredients to serve 6
6 poached eggs
6 toasted croûtons
½ oz. butter
½ oz. plain flour
¼ pint veal or chicken stock
¼ pint milk
salt and pepper
2 egg yolks
½ cup grated cheese
¼ cup butter
½ pound tender asparagus

Preparation

Melt the butter in the saucepan and stir in the flour. Stir this roux over gentle heat for a few minutes until the flour is partially cooked but not browned. Remove the pan from the heat and gradually pour in the milk. Slowly add the stock, stirring constantly to prevent the sauce from becoming lumpy. Add the two egg yolks which have been beaten lightly. Lastly, add the ½ cup grated cheese.

Pour the sauce over 6 poached eggs, each set on a croûton on an oval platter. Brown for a minute under the grill.

Serve with asparagus stalks that are sauteed lightly in butter and gathered in small bouquets. The eggs on toast are separated by the asparagus spears cut in 4–5 inch lengths. Mushrooms browned in butter and seasoned with paprika may be mounded in the centre of the dish.

Mrs. Lawson Johnson

Barquettes d'Oeuf

Ingredients to serve 6
2 eggs
3 oz. flour
1 tablespoon olive oil
1 pint water
½ pint Béchamel sauce
2 oz. grated Cheddar and Parmesan cheese
6 hard boiled eggs
salt
¼ cup double cream

Preparation
Make a batter of the two eggs, lightly beaten, 3 oz. flour, olive oil and water. Dip a mould into this batter and fry until golden brown, repeating until the number of moulds required are fried.

Heat ½ pint Béchamel sauce. Add all but 2 tablespoons of the grated cheese and stir until well blended. Add the hard boiled eggs, chopped evenly, and salt to taste.

Fill the moulds with the mixture. Mix a little grated cheese that was reserved, with the double cream. Cover the centres of the moulds with the cheese cream and brown for three to five minutes under the grill. Garnish with parsley, and serve bubbling hot.

Mrs. McGuiness,
Cook to Lady Hothfield

Oeufs Piquants

Ingredients to serve 4
 4 eggs
1½ oz. breadcrumbs
 1 tablespoon chopped
    parsley
    salt
    pepper
1½ oz. butter
 1 cup button
    mushrooms
 1 tablespoon oil
    lemon juice
    Sauce Espagnole,
    optional

Preparation
Boil three of the eggs until hard. Allow to cool before shelling. Put in refrigerator for half an hour to chill, making them easier to slice. Put each egg through an egg slicer for neat, uniform slices. Set aside.

Mix breadcrumbs, parsley, salt and pepper together. Beat the remaining egg, and dip the egg slices first in the beaten egg, then in the seasoned breadcrumbs. Handle the slices carefully so they do not tear apart. Fry in the butter which has reached the bubbling point, for a few minutes on each side. It may be easier to turn the slices with two spatulas.

Fry mushrooms in oil and fill the centre of an au gratin dish, arranging the fried egg slices around them. Sprinkle lemon juice over the top, and garnish with watercress.

If desired, a sauceboat of Sauce Espagnole may be served separately.

Mrs. Fraser,
Cook to Philip Hodgson, Esq.

Eggs à la Boston

Ingredients to serve 2
$\frac{3}{4}$ oz. butter
1 tablespoon chopped
  onion
1 teaspoon flour
$\frac{1}{8}$ pint milk
1 oz. chopped ham
3 eggs
  pepper
  salt
  nutmeg
2 tablespoons finely
  chopped ham

Preparation
Fry onion in the butter until it just turns pale brown in colour. Add the flour and milk. Cook this sauce until thick, stirring occasionally. Allow to cool.

Separate the eggs. Reserve the whites. Beat the yolks into the white sauce, and add the ham and seasonings. Beat the egg whites until stiff. Fold egg whites into the sauce.

Pour mixture into a greased fireproof dish and sprinkle the finely chopped ham on top. Bake in moderately high oven (400°F, Mark 6) until the top is pale brown and the eggs have firmly set. The eggs should puff up slightly. Serve very hot.

The Lady Wraxall

Soufflé d'Oeufs Claridge's

Ingredients to serve 4
Boned breast meat from a chicken
2 tablespoons butter
$\frac{3}{4}$ cup double cream
salt, pepper, paprika, cayenne pepper
6 eggs
1 pound young asparagus spears
4 tablespoons butter
Parmesan mixture:
5 oz. flour
12 oz. boiled milk
salt
pepper
nutmeg
2 oz. grated Parmesan cheese
1 oz. butter
4 egg yolks
4 egg whites

Preparation
Take the white meat from the breast of a chicken which has been poached. For a variation of flavour, the chicken can be poached in chicken stock and wine. Cut the meat into small medallions and fry lightly in butter. Reduce the cream by one-quarter and add to the poultry. Season well and place medallions in sauce on earthenware au gratin dish.

Poach the eggs lightly (2 minutes) and drain well. Lay the eggs on the chicken. Between each egg lay the asparagus in small bunches. The asparagus stalks should be cooked for 7 minutes, tossed lightly in butter and cut in 4-inch spears.

Prepare the Parmesan mixture: Mix flour with boiled milk. Season and bring again to the boil, stirring constantly. Remove from fire and add the cheese, butter and yolks. At the last, add the egg whites, stiffly beaten.

Cover the eggs and chicken medallions with the Parmesan mixture. Bake in moderate oven (350°F, Mark 4) for 6 minutes being sure the eggs are not overdone.

Claridge's, London

Filling for Egg Tartlets

Ingredients to serve 4
1 onion
$\frac{1}{4}$ **pound mushrooms**
1 oz. butter
  salt, pepper
1 tablespoon chopped
  parsley
1 tablespoon plain
  flour
$\frac{1}{4}$ **pint milk**
4 tartlets
4 eggs
1 oz. grated Cheddar,
  Edam or
  Emmentaler cheese

Preparation
Peel and chop the onion finely. Skin the mushrooms and chop both the cup and stalk into dice. Melt the butter in a saucepan. Add the onion and mushrooms and cook gently until both are soft, but not brown.

Add the salt, pepper, and parsley; stir in flour gradually. Slowly add the milk, stirring constantly until the mixture thickens. Continue to cook, stirring, for another three minutes. Fill each tartlet with mixture and keep warm.

Poach the eggs for 3–4 minutes. Place an egg in each tartlet and sprinkle the tops with cheese. Brown lightly under the grill. Serve sprinkled with paprika.

The Marchioness of Cambridge

Oeufs Brouillés Hongroise

Ingredients to serve 4
2 onions
2 tablespoons butter
4 small carrots
1 teaspoon flour
$\frac{1}{2}$ teaspoon tomato purée
 salt
 pepper
$\frac{1}{3}$ pint stock
$\frac{1}{4}$ pound small sausages
5 eggs
6 small toast croûtons, buttered
 pimientoes

Preparation

Cut two onions into quarters and brown in butter. Scrape the carrots and cut into olive shapes. Add the onions and butter. Brown lightly. Stir in 1 teaspoon flour, the tomato puree and the seasonings.

Cook for 5 minutes over medium heat. Add $\frac{1}{3}$ pint stock, stirring until blended. Simmer until the vegetables are tender, about 25 minutes. Add $\frac{1}{4}$ pound small sausages five minutes before the vegetables have cooked through. The tiny, spicy sausages available in delicatessans give a special flavour to this dish.

Butter 5 ramekins and heat two minutes in fairly hot oven. Break an egg into each ramekin, season, and bake for 4–5 minutes. Place the croûtons on a platter. Pour the vegetable sauce over top. Sprinkle with pimientoes cut in strips. Place the eggs around the outside of the dish. Reheat for a few minutes if necessary.

Mrs. Williams

Egg Mousse

Ingredients to serve 4
7 eggs
$\frac{1}{2}$ pint double cream
1 teaspoon anchovy
  essence
1 teaspoon Worcester
  sauce
  salt
  pepper
1 oz. gelatine
Aspic:
2 cups stock
$\frac{1}{4}$ pint sherry
1 tablespoon vinegar
2 oz. gelatine
2 egg whites

Preparation
Boil the eggs until hard. Plunge into cold water. When cold, shell, and press through a sieve.

Be sure the cream is very cold. Whisk the cream until thoroughly whipped. Add to the eggs with the anchovy essence, Worcester sauce and seasonings. Melt 1 oz. gelatine and blend into mixture. Place in refrigerator for about 20 minutes. When the mixture is nearly cold, pour into a souffle dish and allow to set firmly.

Decorate with aspic jelly: place the cold stock, sherry, and vinegar in a large saucepan. Add the gelatine and heat slowly over a gentle heat, stirring occasionally. Whisk the egg whites until frothy, adding them one at a time to the saucepan. Whisk over low heat until boiling, then remove from heat; set pan on to boil again and repeat process twice. Strain through several thicknesses of muslin. The aspic, when set, can be cut into various shapes.

The Marchioness of Cambridge

Fish

Madras Fish The Marchioness of Cambridge
Haddock Monte Carlo The Savoy Hotel, London
Croûtons of Finnan Haddock The Lady Maud Carnegie
Kipper Soufflé Mrs. Andrews, Cook to Mrs. Oliver Martin-Smith
Mousse de Merluche Their Majesties
King George VI and Queen Elizabeth
Chartreuse of Salmon Mrs. Lawson Johnson
Filet de Sole Miss Grace Moore Claridge's, London
Filet of Sole Duglère Alfred Cross, Chef of Crockford's
Truite Île de France Monsieur Pierre, Proprietaire et Chef de
Cuisine, Grand Hôtel de France et d'Angleterre, Beauvais
Truite au Chambertin Monsieur Pierre, Proprietaire et Chef de
Cuisine, Grand Hôtel de France et d'Angleterre, Beauvais
Suprême de Turbot à la Dresde M. Gurney, c/o Mrs. Churchill Hale
Turbotin Bonne Femme Mrs. Laurence Carr
Filets aux Champignons The Marchioness of Cambridge
Crab Meat Remick Joseph Boggia, The Plaza, New York
Petits Homards Duchesse Their Majesties
King George VI and Queen Elizabeth

Madras Fish

Ingredients to serve 4
2 tablespoons oil
1 onion
2 tomatoes
1 heaped teaspoon
   curry powder
$\frac{1}{2}$ cup sultanas
1 pound cod or
   haddock
1 cup boiled rice
$\frac{1}{2}$ oz. butter
2 tablespoons cream
   salt
2 hard-boiled eggs

Preparation

Chop the onion into small dice and fry in oil to a golden-brown. Chop the tomatoes into eighths. Add to the onions. Toss in curry powder and sultanas. Simmer just until the sultanas are cooked, not more than five minutes.

Flake the fish. Carefully fold into the curry mixture. Mix the butter, cream and salt with the boiled rice. It is preferable to blend the butter in a melted or at least softened form.

Combine with the curried fish. Reheat in moderately high oven (400°F, Mark 5) until bubbling. Slice the eggs in an egg slicer so the pieces are evenly cut. Place the egg slices around the curried fish and serve with an assortment of condiments, including chutney, green pepper, and sliced bananas.

The Marchioness of Cambridge

Haddock Monte Carlo

Ingredients to serve 4
2 one-pound smoked
haddock
1 pint water
4 tomatoes
4 oz. butter
1 pint cream
freshly ground
pepper

Preparation
Fillet two nice smoked haddock of one pound each in weight. Set aside.

Bring the water to a boil in a saucepan. With slotted spoon, put the tomatoes in the water and blanch for 15 seconds. Remove and skin. Slice the tomatoes, taking care to remove the pips.

Put the fillets in a buttered earthenware dish with the tomatoes. Add the pint of fresh cream and four ounces of butter, softened, distributing the butter and cream over the fillets. Grind fresh pepper over the top.

Bake in a hot oven (425°F, Mark 7) for ten minutes. Serve at once garnished with parsley.

The Savoy Hotel, London

Croûtons of Finnan Haddock

Ingredients to serve 6
½ **pound smoked
   haddock**
3 anchovies
**1 ounce butter or
   margarine**
   salt
   pepper
   thyme
**1 tablespoon milk or
   cream**
**1 teaspoon lemon
   juice**
**6 small round
   croûtons of fried
   bread**
1 hard boiled egg
1 lemon
   **cayenne pepper,
   freshly ground**

Preparation
Either cooked or uncooked haddock may be used. If the fish is uncooked, dip it into boiling water and remove the skin and bone. Skin and bone the anchovies also, and chop the anchovies lightly.

Flake the flesh of the haddock and pound with the anchovies in a mortar. As the fish begins to break down, pound in the butter or margarine. Add the seasonings, and blend. Rub the fish through a wire sieve until it is of the proper consistency. Add the milk and lemon juice.

Heat the mixture through, but do not let it boil. Mound the fish on the croutons of fried bread. Separate the hard boiled yolk and rub it through a clean sieve, sprinkling the yolk over the croutons. Cut the lemon into pinwheel shapes and use to decorate the croutons. Any other dried or smoked fish may be substituted.

The Lady Maud Carnegie

Kipper Soufflé

Ingredients to serve 4
1 oz. butter
1 oz. flour
$\frac{1}{4}$ pint milk
2 kippers
2 eggs, separated
salt and pepper to taste
$\frac{3}{4}$ cup milk
1 oz. butter
1 oz. flour

Preparation

Melt 1 oz. butter in a saucepan and add 1 oz. flour. Cook for 2 minutes, but do not let the roux brown. Add $\frac{1}{4}$ pint milk and cook until the mixture leaves the sides and bottom of the pan clean. Remove from fire and cover. Trim the kippers, setting the trimmings aside to make the sauce.

Sieve the flesh to make 3 oz. Add the sieved kippers to the white sauce. Stir well; stir in the egg yolks one at a time. Season to taste. Whisk the two egg whites until stiff. Add to the mixture, carefully folding in, and not overmixing.

Put into a well-buttered souffle mould. Cover the top with greased paper to prevent the water from dripping on the surface. Steam gently for half to three-quarters of an hour. Turn out and serve with the following sauce poured around: Soak the kipper trimmings in milk for 20 minutes. Melt 1 oz. butter and add 1 oz. flour and enough flavoured milk to make a thick creamy sauce.

Mrs. Andrews,
Cook to Mrs. Oliver Martin-Smith

Mousse de Merluche

Ingredients to serve 6
- **6 merluche (hake or haddock may be substituted)**
- **salt**
- **pepper**
- **2 tablespoons Béchamel sauce**
- **2 egg whites**
- **paprika**
- **$\frac{3}{4}$-1 cup cream**

Preparation

Fillet and skin 6 Merluche weighing $\frac{3}{4}$ pound each. From the thick part of the fillet, cut two or three medallions of the same size. Place the trimmings on one side for later use as the sauce base. Lightly poach the medallions in a good court bouillon.

Pound the trimmings well in a mortar with salt and pepper. Add 2 tablespoons thick Béchamel sauce, and mix well. Fold in the whites of two eggs which have been beaten slightly, adding one at a time. Blend the mixture well.

Pass the whole mixture through a fine sieve and refrigerate for 25 minutes. Add the cream until the mixture reaches a smooth, fairly thick consistency. Correct seasoning if necessary, and refrigerate.

Decorate the mousse with radishes and peppers in flower patterns laid on the medallions and set around the mousse. Serve quite cold.

Their Majesties King George VI and Queen Elizabeth

58

Chartreuse of Salmon

Ingredients to serve 4
1 cup boiled salmon
¼ cup cracker
   (biscuit) crumbs
   dash of cayenne
    pepper
½ teaspoon salt
½ teaspoon sharp
   mustard
   juice of ½ lemon
2 eggs
2 tablespoons milk or
   cream
Hollandaise sauce:
   juice of ½ lemon
1 teaspoon water
2 egg yolks
4 oz. butter
   salt
   cayenne pepper

Preparation
Mince the salmon and place in a bowl. Add the salt, cayenne, mustard, lemon juice, and cracker crumbs. Separate the eggs, reserving the whites. Moisten the salmon with the yolks of the eggs, and if the fish is very dry, add two tablespoons of milk or cream. Blend thoroughly.

Beat the egg whites until stiff and fold into the salmon mixture. Put into buttered ramekins or custard cups. Set them in a pan of hot water and bake for 20 minutes in a moderate oven (350°F, Mark 4).

While the salmon is cooking, make the hollandaise sauce: place the lemon juice and water in a small bowl. Set the bowl over a saucepan of simmering water. Add the egg yolks and ½ oz. butter, stirring with a whisk all the time so the mixture doesn't curdle. Continue to whisk; take off heat and add the butter in small bits, whisking well all the time. Season with salt and cayenne pepper. Pass the sauce round in a sauceboat, or pour around the salmon and garnish.

Mrs. Lawson Johnson

Filet de Sole
Miss Grace Moore

Ingredients to serve 4

2 potatoes
4 medium sized
  artichoke hearts
3½ oz. small fresh
  morels, if available
salt
pepper
paprika
fresh chervil
3 tablespoons butter
4 fillets of sole
4 tablespoons butter
2 tomatoes
4 tablespoons oil
pinch pounded
  parsley
pinch chervil
1 teaspoon ketchup
  or Worcester sauce
juice of ½ lemon

Preparation

Dice two potatoes into equal sized bits. Cut the four medium-sized artichoke hearts into the same size. Add 3½ oz. small fresh morels. If the morels are not available, substitute with the golden variety of small mushrooms called pfefferlings. Clean them well. Season to taste and fry each vegetable separately in butter. Fresh herbs will improve the flavour of the dish.

Cut up four fillets of sole into large julienne strips. Season and fry in butter. Slice the tomatoes fairly thick and season. Heat oil until it is smoking. Fry tomatoes until lightly browned. Remove and drain.

Just before serving, stir the fillets for a few seconds. Arrange in an earthenware dish. Garnish the dish with the tomato slices, pinch of pounded parsley, and chervil; add the ketchup or Worcester sauce. Squeeze the juice of half a lemon over top. Dot with nut-sized pats of butter. Brown in moderate oven and serve very hot.

Claridge's, London

Filet of Sole Duglère

Ingredients to serve 4
4 fillets of sole
  salt
  pepper
  dash fresh thyme
    and rosemary
6 tomatoes
1 shallot
½ cup white wine
½ cup cream
¼ pound butter
  parsley
  lemon and green
    pepper garnish

Preparation
Place the sole in a buttered dish and season with the herbs. Blanch the tomatoes by dipping in boiling water for 12–15 seconds, and skin them. Cut the tomatoes in half and take out the pips. Cut into small dice.

Chop the shallot and sprinkle over the sole with the tomatoes. Pour the half-cup white wine over the fish. Cover the dish with greased paper and cook for seven or eight minutes in fairly hot oven (400°F, Mark 6). Keep fish warm.

Scrape the tomatoes off and place in a small saucepan with the liquor from the fish. Add the cream and cook over medium heat. Reduce the liquid for several minutes. Add the parsley, well chopped; then gradually mix in the softened butter, shaking the pan to mix gently. Cover fish with sauce and garnish with wedges of lemon, decoratively cut, and green pepper strips.

Alfred Cross,
Chef of Crockford's

Truite Île de France

Ingredients to serve 4
1 fresh trout
1 cup mushrooms
$\frac{1}{4}$ cup mixed fresh
fines herbes
$\frac{1}{4}$ cup breadcrumbs
pinch nutmeg
cayenne pepper
2 tablespoons cream
$\frac{1}{4}$ pound butter
juice of half a lemon
2 lemons
toasted almonds

Preparation

Clean trout, preferably one that has been freshly caught. Stuff with a forcemeat, made from the following combination: Chop the mushrooms very finely, in duxelle. Mix with fresh fines herbes and breadcrumbs, which have been seasoned with salt, pepper, and herbs. Add a pinch of nutmeg and cayenne. Bind mixture together with enough fresh cream to give it the proper consistency. Double cream may be preferable, depending upon the thickness desired.

Coat the trout with a good layer of softened butter which has been mixed with the fresh lemon juice. Bake for 20 minutes at (350°F, Mark 4), basting frequently. When the butter is completely absorbed, serve garnished with lemon cups, tomatoes and small prawns.

Monsieur Pierre,
Proprietaire et Chef de Cuisine,
Grand Hôtel de France
et d'Angleterre, Beauvais

Truite au Chambertin

Ingredients to serve 4
- **4 small trout**
- **10 rashers thinly sliced bacon**
- **10 very small onions**
- **4 small carrots bouquet garni**
- **$\frac{1}{2}$ pint Burgundy, preferably a good Chambertin**
- **$\frac{1}{2}$ pint water**

Preparation

Carefully clean 4 small trout. Butter a fairly large casserole, which is flame-proof. Brown several thin strips of bacon, slowly, so they do not burn. Add the onions as the bacon begins to brown.

Make a bouquet garni in double muslin of parsley, thyme, bay leaf, 2 pepper-corns, and a pinch of mace, if desired. Slice the carrots in strips and add to casserole. Partially cook the vegetables slowly. Lay the trout on top and cover with the equal amounts of Burgundy wine and water.

Cook gently until the trout are nicely poached. Remove them and place on a serving platter. Keep warm on a corner of the stove or in a warming oven. Gently reduce the liquor remaining in the casserole. Cover the trout with a rich hollandaise sauce (see page 59 for hollandaise recipe), finally adding the reduced liquor just before serving.

Monsieur Pierre,
Proprietaire et Chef de Cuisine,
Grand Hôtel de France
et d'Angleterre, Beauvais

Suprême de Turbot à la Dresde

Ingredients to serve 4

4 turbot fillets
1 teaspoon butter
¼ cup mushrooms
¼ cup cooked lobster
salt
cayenne pepper
2 teaspoons lemon juice
6 oz. grated Gruyère or Emmentaler cheese
4 tablespoons double cream
2 teaspoons English mustard
½ cup lobster or shrimp sauce

Preparation

Flatten out the fillets of turbot well with a wet chopping knife. Arrange the fillets in a lightly buttered flat au gratin dish on which the fish will be served. Put the skinned side of the fish on the bottom. Sprinkle the top with finely chopped raw mushrooms.

Chop the lobster into fine bits, or shred. Add to the fish with salt, cayenne pepper and lemon juice. Or use corraline pepper if available as a substitute for the cayenne. Cover the fish with buttered brown paper. Bake in moderate oven (350°F, Mark 4) for 25 minutes. While fish is cooking, make the mustard sauce:

Mix 6 oz. grated cheese with 4 tablespoons thick cream and the English mustard. Stir over low heat until the cheese is melted and well blended with the other ingredients.

When the fish is cooked, mask the fillets with the mustard cheese sauce and brown quickly under the grill. Bring the lobster or shrimp sauce to the boiling point. Pour around the edge of the dish and garnish with fresh cress.

M. Gurney,
c/o Mrs. Churchill Hale

Turbotin Bonne Femme

Ingredients to serve 4
- **one 2½-3 pound chicken turbot**
- **1 teaspoon butter**
- **1 tablespoon chopped shallots**
- **pinch chopped parsley**
- **3 oz. fresh mushrooms**
- **½ cup white wine**
- **⅓ pint fish stock**
- **3 tablespoons cream**
- **3 oz. butter**

Preparation

The chicken turbot is the more tender, white variety of turbot. If not available, use an ordinary turbot. Clean the turbot and make an incision down the middle of the back.

Sprinkle over the bottom of a buttered tray the shallots, finely chopped, and a pinch of coarsely chopped parsley. Slice the mushrooms very thin. Place the turbot in the tray, moisten with the white wine and a third of a pint of fresh stock. Cook gently in the oven (325°F, Mark 3) and baste frequently.

When cooked, dish up the turbot and keep warm. Pour the cooking liquid into a saute pan. Reduce it by half and gradually add three tablespoons of cream and 3 oz. butter. Pour the sauce over the turbot, garnish, and glaze quickly under a grill or in a very hot oven.

Mrs. Laurence Carr

Filets aux Champignons

Ingredients to serve 4
- 4 **fillets of sole or whiting**
- ½ **pound fresh mushrooms**
- 2 **oz. butter**
- 4 **tablespoons chopped onion**
- 2 **teaspoons chopped parsley**
- 4-5 **tomatoes**
- **fresh breadcrumbs**
- 1 **oz. butter melted with 1 tablespoon oil**
- **fresh lemon slices**

Preparation

Skin and prepare the fish. Season each fillet with pepper, salt and lemon juice. Fold each one over and secure with a toothpick if necessary. Place fillets in a greased flameproof dish with a tablespoon of water. Cover with buttered paper and bake in a moderate oven for 12 minutes.

Put an ounce of butter into a small saucepan. Add the chopped onion and mushrooms. Season with pepper and salt. Cook until tender, about 8–10 minutes, adding more butter if necessary and tossing lightly to coat the mixture. Add the parsley.

Pile the fish in the centre of a flameproof dish so that they make a slope toward the edge. Sprinkle with breadcrumbs and pour the oiled butter evenly over the fish. Cut the tomatoes in quarters, and make a circle of tomatoes around the edge with one tomato in the centre, not cut completely through, to form an open flower form. Brown in hot oven or under the grill. Serve in the dish it was cooked in with slices of fresh lemon, cut very thin, between the tomatoes.

The Marchioness of Cambridge

Crab Meat Remick

Ingredients to serve 4
- **1 teaspoon English mustard**
- **½ teaspoon paprika**
- **pinch celery salt**
- **dash Tabasco sauce**
- **1 cup Chili sauce**
- **1 quart mayonnaise**
- **dash tarragon vinegar**
- **salt**
- **pepper**
- **2 pounds back fin crab meat**
- **4 slices bacon**
- **¼ cup Parmesan cheese**

Preparation

Put one teaspoon English mustard, ½ teaspoon paprika, pinch of celery salt, and the dash of Tabasco sauce into a mixing bowl, blending well. Add the Chili sauce, one quart of mayonnaise, and a dash of Tarragon vinegar. Mix well together; season to taste. Set the sauce aside.

Select the best crab meat and flake in fairly large pieces. Set in open clam shell or scallop shells. Soft clams or oysters may be substituted for the crab meat if preferred. If oysters or soft clams are used, they must be poached before using, just until tender. Proceed as with the crab meat.

Heat the crab meat in a moderate oven. When it is warm, about 15 minutes, cover with strips of bacon that have been cooked until lightly brown. Coat with the Remick sauce. Sprinkle grated Parmesan cheese over the top and brown under grill about 4 minutes.

Joseph Boggia,
The Plaza, New York

Petits Homards Duchesse

Ingredients to serve 4
**4 lobsters, weighing
$\frac{3}{4}$ lbs. each
3 pints court bouillion
4 eggs, separated
$\frac{1}{2}$ cup grated
Parmesan cheese
$\frac{1}{2}$ cup browned
breadcrumbs
$\frac{2}{3}$ cup melted butter**
Sauce Americaine:
**2 large lobsters, about
$1\frac{1}{2}$-2 pounds each
seasoning
2 oz. each, butter and
oil
4 chopped shallots
$\frac{2}{3}$ pint white wine
4 tablespoons tomato
purée
pinch parsley
2 oz. butter**

Preparation
First prepare the lobster Americaine sauce: Carefully crack the pieces of lobster and extract meat. Season and cook in 1 oz. oil and butter. Add shallots, wine, parsley, and tomato purée. Simmer 20 minutes. Add the chopped coral and intestines of lobster, and 1 oz. butter. Reduce liquid to half and strain.

Prepare the small lobsters by poaching in a good court bouillion for 12 minutes. Chill; cut each lobster lengthwise from head to tail. Take out the meat and clean thoroughly in warm salted water. Dry in a clean towel.

Cut the claw meat into small dice. The tail meat has to be chopped as it is tougher. Wash the carcasses well, and dry. Cover with melted butter and arrange on a baking sheet.

The Americaine sauce should now be ready to blend with the meat. Add one yolk of egg at a time. Whip 2 of the egg whites until very stiff. Fold the egg whites carefully into the lobster. Fill the carcasses level with the edge of the shell. Sprinkle the tops with the combined grated cheese and breadcrumbs. Brush over with melted butter and cook for an additional 7 minutes in hot oven (425°F, Mark 7) just before serving.

**Their Majesties King George VI
and Queen Elizabeth**

Poultry

Poulet au Gourmet Kensington Palace
Southern Fried Chicken Clark Gable
Poulet Sauté au Vin Rouge Mrs. Laurence Carr
Poulet Sauté Chevreuse Monsieur Avignon, Chef of the
Ritz Hotel, London
Emincé de Volaille à la King The Berkeley Hotel, London
Poulet Princesse Mrs. Williams
Chicken Vieux Maison The Marchioness of Cambridge
Poulet Sauté Aperitif L'Aperitif Grill, London
Spatchcock of Chicken or Pheasant Mrs. Ian Erskine
Paella à la Criolla Count Jarisch
Canard à l'Orange Lady Dynoven
Filets de Canard Suprême King's Guard, St. James's Palace
Pulled and Grilled Pheasant H.R.H. Princess Marina,
Duchess of Kent
Pheasant Cutlets H.R.H. Princess Marina, Duchess of Kent
Turkey Stuffing Mrs. Lawson Johnson

Poulet au Gourmet

Ingredients to serve 4
**1 chicken, weighing
  3-4 pounds
  ground sage
  salt
  paprika
  breadcrumbs
3 tablespoons
  vegetable oil
½ cup white wine
4 tomatoes
1 tin anchovy fillets
1 small tin ripe
  olives
1-2 cups chicken broth**

Preparation
Cut the chicken into pieces with kitchen scissors. Season and coat with breadcrumbs. Fry in oil until the chicken is a light brown colour. Place pieces in a casserole large enough to hold all the pieces in one layer.

Pour half a cup of wine into the oil and heat to deglaze the pan. Add tomatoes cut into quarters, the anchovies and ripe olives, stoned and drained.

Cook for 5 minutes and add to the chicken in the casserole. Add just enough chicken broth or water to cover the chicken. Cover the casserole and bake in a moderate oven (350°F, Mark 4) for about one hour. Uncover and cook for an additional ½ hour to reduce liquid. Serve in baking dish.

Kensington Palace

Southern Fried Chicken

Ingredients to serve 4
3 pound frying chicken
½ cup shortening
salt
1 teaspoon powdered thyme
¼ cup water
½ tablespoon plain flour
½ teaspoon salt
⅛ teaspoon pepper
½ teaspoon paprika
1 cup boiling water
2 tablespoons cream
½ cup button mushrooms

Preparation
Cut chicken into serving pieces. Heat shortening; roll each piece of chicken in flour, season with salt and thyme, and fry in shortening. Brown on all sides. Reduce heat to medium and add ¼ cup water; cover and cook for 15 minutes. Turn pieces and cook for an additional 10 minutes or until chicken is tender.

Remove pieces to heated platter. Pour off all the fat from the pan except 2 tablespoons. Add 1 tablespoon flour, blend and stir, deglazing the pan. As the gravy base browns, add salt, pepper, paprika, and boiling water. Cook until gravy is smooth and thickened, stirring constantly. Add the cream and blend. Pour around the chicken. Garnish with button mushrooms browned in some of the leftover chicken fat.

Clark Gable

Poulet Sauté au Vin Rouge

Ingredients to serve 4

**1 whole chicken,
about 3 pounds
4 tablespoons flour
salt
pepper
paprika
4 rashers bacon
½ cup small white
onions
3 tablespoons oil
2 tablespoons butter
½ cup red Bordeaux
wine
½ cup brandy
2 shallots
bouquet garni of bay
leaf, parsley, lemon
thyme
3 leaves tarragon
dash grated nutmeg
2 tablespoons
Espagnole sauce
1 tablespoon chopped
parsley**

Preparation

Cut up the chicken into serving pieces. Season with salt, pepper and paprika and coat with flour. Using a fireproof casserole, fry the cubes of bacon and button onions in combined oil and butter. Saute the chicken in the pan with bacon and onions.

Dice shallots. Drain off the fat and add ½ cup wine, brandy and shallots. Add the bouquet garni, and distribute a few tarragon leaves over the top. Grate nutmeg over chicken and bring the liquid in the pan to a boil. At this point, set the casserole, covered, in a moderate pre-heated oven and bake for 20 minutes.

When the chicken is tender, remove tarragon leaves and lift each piece of chicken to a heated platter. Arrange the bacon and onions around the chicken. To the juices in the pan, add 2 tablespoons Espagnole or other rich brown sauce. When heated through, pour sauce over chicken and sprinkle with chopped parsley.

Mrs. Laurence Carr

Poulet Sauté Chevreuse

Ingredients to serve 4
2 poussins
¼ pound butter
  salt
  pepper
1 cup white port
½ pound fresh
  mushrooms
1 quart fresh cream

Preparation
It is preferable to use poussins, the young, tender chickens weighing 1–2 pounds. If not available, select a young tender chicken of 3–3½ pounds in weight. Cut into small neat serving pieces. The success of this dish depends on its cooking on a very low heat. Heat ¼ pound butter in frying pan over low heat. It must not be allowed to brown. Put the pieces of chicken in the hot butter, cover the frying pan and cook gently for ½ hour. Add pepper and salt, and 1 cup white port and cook for another half hour.

Wash and dry ½ pound small white mushrooms. Do not peel or slice them. Add the mushrooms to the chicken and cook for 15 minutes. Add one quart of fresh cream to the sauce and continue cooking over low heat another 12 minutes, or until the cream has had a chance to thicken slightly and is hot and simmering.

Monsieur Avignon,
Chef of the Ritz Hotel, London

Emincé de Volaille à la King

Ingredients to serve 3

1 boiling chicken, about 3½ pounds
2 carrots
1 leek
2 stalks celery, with leaves
1 medium onion
bouquet garni
2 teaspoons salt
white pepper
small bunch parsley
salt
cayenne pepper
⅔ cup cream
3 egg yolks
⅓ cup sherry
¼ cup pimientoes
1 truffle

Preparation

Cover the chicken, seasonings, and bouquet garni with boiling water. Add carrots, leek, celery, onion, and cook for 8 minutes. Reduce heat to low and simmer for one hour. Lift the chicken from the stock and allow to cool slightly. Remove the legs and breast; bone the breast carefully with a sharp knife. Cut the breast and leg meat into scallops and place in a small saute pan. Add enough cream to cover, and salt and cayenne and heat through.

While the chicken is heating, put 3 egg yolks in a clean saucepan with the sherry. Whisk briskly near the burner, but not over the heat, until the yolks form a thick cream, without bubbling. Care should be taken not to overheat the yolks. Slowly stir the egg sauce into the cream, moving the chicken pieces to one side of the saute pan. Add ⅔ of the pimientoes, cut in julienne strips. Serve with slices of truffles and the remaining pimientoes in a spoke form on the creamed chicken. Serve croûtons or bouchées or puff pastry separately.

The Berkeley Hotel, London

Poulet Princesse

Ingredients to serve 4
**one 3½-4 pound roast-
ing chicken**
2 teaspoons butter
2 leeks, sliced
3 carrots
  bouquet garni
**¼ cup white
  Bordeaux wine**
½ cup chicken stock
2 cucumbers
2 teaspoons butter
**1 teaspoon chopped
  parsley**
**½ teaspoon chopped
  fresh basil**
6 tomatoes
**½ teaspoon chopped
  mint**
¼ pound mushrooms
**1 teaspoon lemon
  juice**
**1 teaspoon tomato
  purée**

Preparation
Using a large, deep roasting pan, brown the chicken in butter over medium heat. Turn it frequently to brown all sides evenly. Add the salt, carrots, leek and a bouquet garni of thyme leaves, parsley, 2 peppercorns and 2 bay leaves. Cook for 3 minutes. Add the wine, stock, and salt to taste. Cover the breast of the chicken with greaseproof paper to keep the flesh from browning too much and roast in moderate oven (350°F, Mark 4) for 45 minutes.

Peel cucumbers and cut into small nut-sized shapes. Blanch for 1 minute; cook in saucepan for 3 minutes in butter. Add basil and parsley. Blanch tomatoes; skin and remove pips, quarter, and add to the cucumbers. Toss with ½ teaspoon mint, sliced mushrooms and another teaspoon butter; cover saucepan and cook over low heat for about 8 minutes. Add lemon juice. Remove chicken and carve into serving pieces. Quickly de-glaze pan; add tomato purée and bring to boiling point. Strain gravy over chicken and garnish with the tomato-cucumber mixture.

Mrs. Williams

Chicken Vieux Maison

Ingredients to serve 4
**one 4-5 pound
  boiling chicken
1 onion
1 chicken cube
¾ oz. butter
¾ oz. plain flour
¼ pint milk
¼ pint clear
  consomme
1-2 cloves garlic
  salt, pepper
  button
    mushrooms
4 vol-au-vent**

Preparation
Put a small onion and a chicken cube inside the bird. Place the chicken in a steamer or a large metal bowl, set in a larger pan of boiling water. Steam for 3–4 hours, refilling the water pan if the water level becomes too low. Melt the butter in a saucepan and stir in the flour. Stir over a gentle heat for a few minutes to cook the flour, never allowing the roux to brown.

Remove the pan from the heat and stir in the milk and stock, a few table-spoons at a time, blending constantly. Return to heat and boil for about 5 minutes. Season with salt and pepper. Add crushed garlic, the amount depend-ing upon individual taste. The sauce should be the consistency of cream.

Cut the chicken in neat slices and cover with the sauce. Serve with small vol-au-vent, filled with mushrooms. Or fry 2 rashers of bacon and crumble, stuffing into split prunes. The prunes are used as a filling for the vol-au-vent instead of button mushrooms.

The Marchioness of Cambridge

Poulet Sauté Aperitif

Ingredients to serve 4

one 3-pound chicken
salt
pepper
3 tablespoons flour
4 tablespoons butter
½ cup Chablis wine
½ cup chicken or
veal stock
4 teaspoons butter
¼ teaspoon basil
salt
pepper
dash lemon juice
½ pound mushrooms
½ pound tomatoes
2 shallots, chopped
6 artichoke hearts
3 large tomatoes
1 tablespoon chopped
parsley

Preparation

Cut chicken into serving pieces; salt and pepper and flour lightly. Heat butter in pan. Turn fire immediately to low, and add the chicken. Cover the pan and cook gently for 6 minutes on each side. Pieces should be golden brown. Remove chicken to warm platter. Over low heat, pour half the wine into the chicken fat and stir, removing the bits of meat clinging to the pan. Reduce the liquid to half. Add the chicken or veal stock and reduce again until of the desired consistency, about 10–15 minutes. Put the chicken pieces back in the sauce and cook, covered, until the chicken is done. Never allow the sauce to boil.

Meanwhile, make the garnishing vegetables. Heat half the butter in a saute pan. Add mushrooms, seasoned with basil, salt, and pepper. At the same time, heat the artichoke hearts in the rest of the butter in a separate pan. Remove mushrooms and add pre-blanched, chopped tomatoes with shallots. Arrange chicken on platter, cover with sauce and surround with vegetables, including the potatoes which are cut in nut shapes and browned in butter.

L'Aperitif Grill, London

Spatchcock of Chicken or Pheasant

Ingredients

**1 spring chicken or
young pheasant**
**2 teaspoons prepared
mustard**
**2 tablespoons
Worcester sauce**
**2 tablespoons
Demarara sugar**
2 tablespoons ketchup
**4 tablespoons chicken
stock**
**6 tablespoons milk or
cream**
**2 teaspoons anchovy
essence or sauce
pinch of red pepper**

Preparation

Split open the chicken or pheasant. Boil
as for Emincé de Volaille (see page 76).
Allow to cool; place in a flat, fire-proof
au gratin dish. Prepare sauce: Combine
mustard, sugar, Worcester sauce and
ketchup. Heat stock; and add the mustard
sauce, stirring until the sauce thickens
slightly. Stir in milk, one tablespoon at a
time.

Add anchovy sauce or quarter amount
if using anchovy essence. Add red pepper. The sauce should be of the consistency to coat the bird. If not thick
enough, allow to cook over low heat to
reduce to the proper consistency.

Pour sauce over split bird and heat in
moderate oven (350°F, Mark 4) until
sauce bubbles slightly, about 12 minutes.

Mrs. Ian Erskine

Paella à la Criolla

Ingredients to serve 4
- **6 chicken breasts**
- **6 chicken legs with thigh joints**
- **6 tablespoons olive oil**
- **$5\frac{1}{2}$ oz. long grain rice**
- **$5\frac{1}{2}$ diced pimientoes**
- **2 oz. fresh peas**
- **4 tomatoes**
- **$3\frac{1}{2}$ oz. crayfish or large prawns, in the shell**
- **$3\frac{1}{2}$ oz. mussels in the shell**
- **generous pinch saffron**
- **$1\frac{1}{2}$ cups chicken stock**

Preparation

Bone the breasts. Cut the leg and thigh joints apart. Saute all chicken pieces in oil, using a large saute or paella pan. Brown chicken about 6 minutes on each side. Combine rice, diced pimientoes and fresh green peas; blend with the chicken pieces.

Cut the tomatoes into eighths and distribute among the chicken. Add the crayfish and mussels, well washed. Sprinkle the saffron around the dish.

Pour boiling chicken stock over the pan. Stir just enough to cover the rice with the boiling liquid and to distribute the saffron. Cover the dish with white buttered paper or aluminium foil and cook for 20–30 minutes or until all liquid is absorbed, over moderate heat. If preferred, the dish may be cooked in the oven. Serve in the same dish.

Count Jarisch

Canard à l'Orange

Ingredients to serve 4
1 duck, weighing
4 pounds
$\frac{1}{2}$ **cup claret or port**
1 orange
salt
pepper
$\frac{1}{2}$ **cup cream**
pinch cayenne
$\frac{1}{2}$ **teaspoon lemon**
juice
1 teaspoon butter

Preparation
Roast duck in fairly hot oven (400°F, Mark 6) allowing 15 minutes per pound. Baste frequently with the juices from the pan. Remove the duck from roasting pan and skin. Keep bird warm.

Drain off fat from the pan and add a half cup of port or claret to the pan. Keep on low heat. Remove skin from the orange; cut into Juliennes and boil for a few minutes to remove the bitter taste. Squeeze the juice from orange into the heating wine.

Cut the meat into fillets and put into the gravy with salt and pepper to taste. Cook over low heat for a few minutes. Transfer fillets to serving dish and keep warm. Pour cream into gravy and bring to a boil, stirring. Reduce gravy by one-third, adding a pinch of cayenne, the lemon juice, and butter.

Just before serving, lay the Julienne oranges over the duck and pour sauce over fillets. If preferred, the duck may be left whole, with the sauce and orange poured over the entire roasted bird.

Lady Dynoven

Filets de Canard Suprême

Ingredients
1 duck with liver
fresh thyme
2-3 tablespoons butter
¼ cup port
salt
pepper
½ teaspoon sage
¼ pint port
6 outer leaves of cos lettuce

Preparation

Roast a wild or Aylesbury duck, laying a piece of fat over the breast of the duck if it is of the wild variety, as these birds tend to be dry. Cool.

Remove the skin and cut the breasts into fillets. Take the duck liver and a few extra livers if available and fry in duck fat with a sprinkling of thyme. When cold, grind the liver together with the meat removed from the remainder of the duck. Add fresh butter to the mixture and mix until creamy. Add port and seasoning to taste.

The forcemeat should be creamy. Press through a fine sieve if necessary. Place forcemeat into a piping bag with a rose pipe and force onto the fillets in a scroll pattern. Refrigerate at least one hour.

Prepare aspic according to the Egg Mousse recipe (see page 50), substituting port for the sherry. Coat the fillets with half the aspic, chopping the other half, when set, and lay on top of lettuce. Top with fillets.

King's Guard, St. James's Palace

Pulled and Grilled Pheasant

Ingredients to serve 4

1 pheasant, ready for the oven
1 oz. butter
6 white peppercorns
1 tablespoon parsley
1 oz. plain flour
¾ pint chicken stock
4 small mushrooms
juice of ½ lemon
salt
1 tablespoon cream
1 egg yolk
½ cup breadcrumbs
1 egg yolk
1 tablespoon butter
1 teaspoon mustard
¼ teaspoon Worcester sauce
¼ teaspoon Harvey sauce

Preparation

Roast pheasant in hot oven (425°F, Mark 7) for 30–60 minutes, depending upon size of the bird. Cool. Cut meat into large thick Juliennes, from all parts of the bird except the legs and wings. Trim the legs and wings. Prepare the suprême sauce:

Melt butter in saucepan; add peppercorns, parsley and flour, stirring constantly. Do not let flour brown. Add stock, stirring, and bring to a boil. Add chopped mushrooms, lemon juice and salt. Simmer gently for 20–25 minutes. Strain, add cream and beaten egg yolk and reheat.

Mix the other egg yolk with butter, mustard, and the Worcester and Harvey sauces. Dip the legs and wings into this mixture, then into breadcrumbs. Bake in a moderate oven for 10 minutes.

To serve, make a division of Duchesse potatoes on a platter, putting the pulled pheasant covered in suprême sauce on one side and the grilled pheasant on the other.

H.R.H. Princess Marina,
Duchess of Kent

Pheasant Cutlets

Ingredients to serve 6

2 **small roast pheasant**
$\frac{1}{2}$ **onion, sliced**
$\frac{1}{2}$ **carrot, sliced**
1 **shallot, chopped**
2 **oz. dripping from roasting pan**
2 **oz. diced bacon**
2 **oz. plain flour**
6 **mushroom stalks**
2 **tablespoons tomato paste**
1 **cup double cream**
2 **tablespoons butter**
2 **tablespoons dry sherry**
  salt
  pepper

Preparation

Remove the meat from the birds. Barely cover the pheasant bones with water, adding the onion, carrot and shallot. Cook slowly with seasoning for 3–4 hours. Strain off stock. Melt dripping in a saucepan. Add bacon and cook until softened. Stir in flour; cook gently 20 minutes. Add 1 pint stock and mushrooms. Simmer for 25 minutes. Add tomato paste, sherry, salt and pepper; strain.

Grind the meat in a mincer and work with mortar and pestle, adding half a pint of the brown sauce and mix well. Whip cream and stir into pheasant. Season to taste.

Butter small cutlet moulds and fill with pheasant mixture. Poach in water for 8 minutes. Slip each cutlet from mould and brown in butter. Arrange the cutlets in a shallow dish, and surround with rice pilaf or brown rice and mushrooms, browned lightly in butter. Serve the remaining brown sauce separately.

H.R.H. Princess Marina,
Duchess of Kent

Turkey Stuffing

Ingredients for a
12–16 pound bird
- **1 turkey liver**
- **12 slices toasted bread**
- **$\frac{1}{4}$ cup butter**
- **3 tablespoons melted lard**
- **1 teaspoon salt**
- **1 teaspoon pepper**
- **1 teaspoon celery seed, crushed**
- **1 teaspoon dried thyme**
- **$\frac{1}{4}$ oz. ground mace**
- **2 tablespoons parsley, finely chopped**
- **$\frac{1}{2}$ oz. nutmeg, freshly grated**
- **2 cups salted pecans**
- **1 cup mushrooms**
- **$\frac{1}{2}$ cup sherry**
- **1 large onion, grated**
- **6 hard boiled eggs**
- **$\frac{1}{2}$ cup boiling water**

Preparation

Boil the liver the day before the stuffing is made and refrigerate. Cut the toasted bread into cubes and place in a large bowl. Chop the liver into dice and add to the bread. Toss with melted butter, lard, and the spices. The pepper and nutmeg are best ground fresh into the stuffing. Chop the pecans in halves. Dice the mushrooms, including stems, and add with the grated onions to the bread cubes. Blend in sherry.

Pour over enough boiling water to moisten. Mix thoroughly with wooden spoon, or with the finger tips when the mixture has cooled enough to handle.

Separate the hard boiled egg yolks and mash. Sieve into stuffing. Press the egg whites through a colander and mix in. When the stuffing is cool, rub the turkey both inside and out with salt and white pepper and fill the neck and body cavities with the stuffing. Roast as usual.

Mrs. Lawson Johnson

Meat

Terrine de Lapereau à la Picarde A. C. Amelot, Chef to
Her Majesty Queen Mary
Kidneys in Red Wine H.R.H. Princess Alice, Countess of Athlone
Flank Steak Roule Claude Rains
Fillets of Beef à l'Espagnole Mrs. Chell, Cook to the
Countess Roberts
Tallarnee Alice Faye
Bitocks à la Russe The Marchioness of Cambridge
Chili con Carne Warner Baxter
Baked Ham The Marchioness of Cambridge
Fried Lamb with Rice and Currant Jelly Jeannette Macdonald
Côte d'Agneau Napolitain Mrs. Williams
Cold Curried Lamb The Cavalry Club
Curried Hot-Pot Colonel Sydney Hankey
West Indian Pepper Pot W. Allen, Chef to Lord Fairhaven
L'Escaloppine de Veau Brownie B. Maccagno, Chef of Luigi's,
London
Veal Escalope Coronation Chef Losano, Nurses Home Kitchen,
London Hospital

Terrine de Lapereau à la Picarde

Ingredients to serve 6

1 rabbit, skinned
freshly ground
pepper
8 slices pickled breast
of pork
2 pounds button
mushrooms
6 carrots
bouquet garni
¾ pint cider
¼ cup brandy
flour
water

Preparation

Joint a rabbit as for stewing and season well with black pepper, freshly ground. Line an eathenware casserole with slices of pickled breast of pork. Place a layer of rabbit on pork. Lay down a layer of button mushrooms, then slices of young carrots. Alternate layers until casserole is full. Add a bouquet garni of parsley, bay leaves, and thyme. Combine brandy and cider. Cover casserole with the liquid.

Heat over moderate fire until just under the boiling point. Seal the top with a fairly thick layer of paste made from flour and water. This is a seal and not to be eaten.

Place casserole in a deep tin, half-filled with water and bake in a moderate oven (350°F, Mark 4) for 1–1½ hours, depending on the age of the rabbit. Remove paste seal. Chicken can be cooked in the same way and served with a layer of chicken jelly on top.

The dish is served on festive occasions in France.

A.C. Amelot,
Chef to Her Majesty Queen Mary

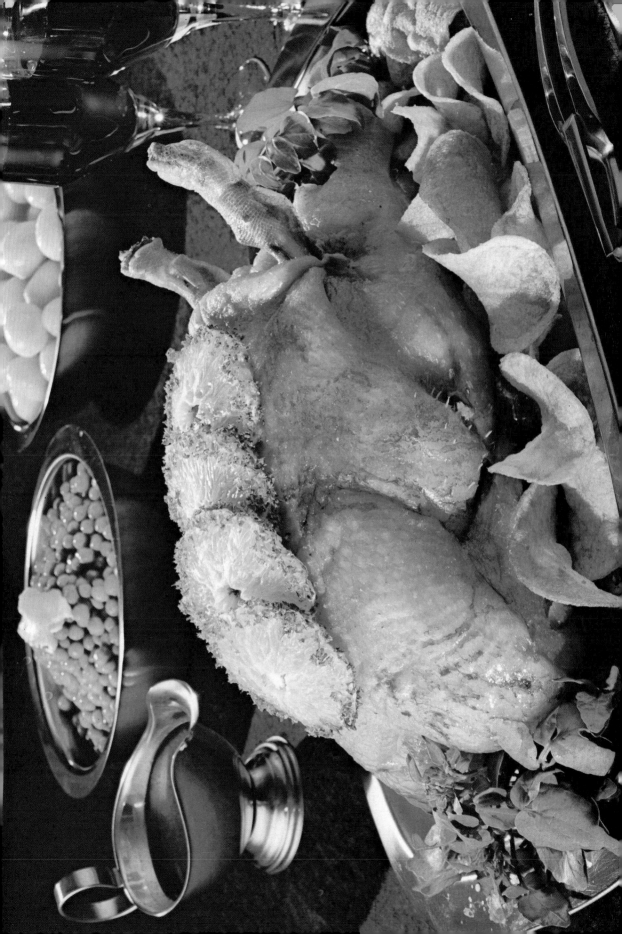

Kidneys in Red Wine

Ingredients to serve 2
- **1 ox kidney**
- **1 large onion, finely chopped**
- **$\frac{3}{4}$ cup red Bordeaux wine**
- **$\frac{3}{4}$ pints of beef stock**
- **$1\frac{1}{2}$ oz. butter**
- **1 teaspoon basil**
- **1 tablespoon tomato purée**
- **1 tablespoon flour**
- **salt**
- **black pepper**

Preparation

Melt the butter in a fire-proof casserole; add the chopped onion and pre-soaked kidney. Cook over gentle heat until onion is soft, but not brown. Remove kidney and keep warm. Remove onion in butter from heat and stir flour into casserole, making a roux. Mix well to absorb the fat. Add the red wine and sufficient stock to cover.

Return the casserole to the heat and stir until sauce has thickened. Add tomato purée and basil. Place covered casserole in the middle of a moderate oven (350°F, Mark 4) and cook for 30 minutes. Serve with buttered rice.

H.R.H. Princess Alice,
Countess of Athlone

Flank Steak Roule

Ingredients to serve 2
2 pounds skirt steak
2 tablespoons butter
1 pound sausage meat
1 onion, finely
   chopped
½ cup chopped celery
   salt
   pepper
2 cups bread crumbs
2 teaspoons chopped
   parsley
1 cup thickened
   homemade vegetable
   soup

Preparation
Have the skirt steak pounded by the butcher. Brown onion in the butter. Put the sausage meat through a sieve. Add to the remaining ingredients, with the drained onion. Mix well.

Spread the surface of the steak with the filling and roll up lengthwise, fastening with skewers and tying securely with string. All the stuffing should be surrounded by the steak, so that none shows when the meat has been rolled and tied.

Add the vegetable stock and ½ cup water, if the stock is not thin enough. Bake in moderate oven (350°F, Mark 4) for 1½ hours or until tender.

Claude Rains

Fillets of Beef à l'Espagnole

Ingredients to serve 2
- **2 fillets of beef**
- **2 oz. butter**
- **2–3 tomatoes**
- **½ teaspoon horseradish**
- **parsley**
- **2½ oz. cream**
- **½ pint aspic jelly, divided in half**
- **2 shallots**
- **salt**
- **pepper**
- **mayonnaise**

Preparation

Cut the fillets into slices about ½-inch thick and the slices into small rounds, all the same size.

Melt the butter in a saute pan; chop shallots and fry lightly in butter. Place the fillets on top and fry over brisk fire until browned on the outside, but still rare in the centres. Remove from the pan and allow to cool.

Whip cream until fairly stiff. Mix with the mayonnaise. Season to taste. Add a little grated fresh horseradish. Arrange fillets on platter and coat with cream mixture. Skin the tomatoes by blanching, and cut into slices. Place a slice on each fillet.

Cover with half of the aspic jelly, half set. Decorate with a little horseradish and chopped parsley in the centre of each fillet. Surround with the remaining aspic which has set completely and has been chopped into dice. Serve cold.

Mrs. Chell,
Cook to the Countess Roberts

Tallarnee

Ingredients to serve 4
1 **medium sized onion,
chopped**
2 **rounded tablespoons
butter**
1 **pound round steak,
ground**
1 **tin tomato purée**
1 **cup water**
2 **rounded cups
uncooked noodles**
1 **tin corn**
1 **tin ripe olives**
1 **cup grated cheese**

Preparation
Fry the onion in the butter until brown.
Add the meat and cook, turning ground
beef until browned through. Pour in
tomato purée and a cup of water. Add
the noodles and stir. Cook over medium
heat for about 6 minutes, or until
noodles are just tender, being careful
they don't stick. If necessary, more water
may be added to keep the mixture moist.
Season to taste. Add the corn and olives.
Pour the mixture into a large buttered
casserole and sprinkle with cheese. Cook
for 30 minutes in a moderate oven (350°F,
Mark 4).

Alice Faye

Bitocks à la Russe

Ingredients
1 pound lean fillet of beef
1 tablespoon chopped parsley
1 teaspoon chopped onion
1 tablespoon cream
1 tablespoon flour
2 tablespoons butter
1–3 teaspoons flour
$\frac{1}{3}$–$\frac{1}{2}$ **cup cream**
3 medium sized onions
$\frac{1}{3}$ **cup vegetable oil**
$\frac{1}{2}$ **cup milk**
2 tablespoons flour

Preparation
Mince one pound lean fillet of beef and put in a bowl together with some parsley and chopped onion. Mix with the cream so the mixture is fairly moist. Make into rounds about $\frac{1}{2}$-inch thick, using a cookie cutter or small bowl edge; the rounds are best made to a uniform shape. Flour lightly and fry in hot butter for about 10 minutes.

Make a sauce from the pan drippings. Add a little cream and flour to the juices until the gravy is of the desired consistency.

Pour some sauce over each bitock and serve the rest in a sauce boat. Garnish with parsley and fried onions.

Make the onions while the bitocks are cooking by separating into rings and dipping first into the milk, then the flour. Heat oil and fry for a few minutes until onions are a golden brown.

The Marchioness of Cambridge

Chili con Carne

Ingredients to serve 6
- 1½ cups olive oil
- 3 medium chopped onions
- 2 pounds ground round steak
- 1 pound ground pork, lean
- 2 tins tomato purée
- 6 cloves garlic
- 3 tablespoons Chili powder
- 2 quarts boiling water
- 3 tablespoons cumin seed
- 3 tablespoons oregano
- 1½ pounds Chili or red kidney beans

Preparation

Soak beans overnight. Cook the following day, covered, in fresh water. Cook slowly over medium heat until beans are tender.

Cook chopped onions in heated olive oil. Simmer for 10 minutes, then add steak and pork. Allow to simmer for another 20 minutes. Stir in the tomato purée, boiling water, Chili powder and crushed garlic. Season to taste.

Make a bouquet garni of oregano and cumin seed. Tie in muslin and add to the meat. The muslin bag will be removed before serving. Mix in the pre-cooked Chili beans. Cover and simmer slowly for 1½ to 2 hours.

Taste at each stage of cooking. The spiciness of the dish can be adjusted by the proportion of Chili powder to liquid. To make a really hot Chili, add Chili capenos while cooking or pass with Chili.

Warner Baxter

Baked Ham

Ingredients to serve 4
- **1 small ham or a boneless bacon hock**
- **$\frac{1}{2}$ cup dark brown sugar**
- **1 tablespoon cloves**
- **$\frac{1}{2}$—$\frac{3}{4}$ cup cider**
- **6 pineapple rings or white peaches**

Preparation

Boil the ham in enough water to cover, allowing a quarter hour per pound of meat. If using bacon hock, allow an extra quarter of an hour. Skin the meat. Press brown sugar over the top. Score the fat lightly. Press cloves at regular intervals into the joint. Place in a baking tin.

Surround with cider and bake in moderate oven (350°F, Mark 4), basting frequently. Add more cider if the meat begins to dry out. If serving hot, put pineapple slices or white peaches in the juice during the last 20 minutes of baking, basting the fruit once. If serving cold, allow to sit until quite cold, for easier slicing.

The Marchioness of Cambridge

Fried Lamb with Rice and Currant Jelly

Ingredients to serve 4
- 1½ **pounds lamb steak**
- 4 **tablespoons butter**
-   **salt**
-   **pepper**
- 1 **teaspoon marjoram**
- ½ **teaspoon thyme**
- ½ **cup current jelly**
- 1 **tablespoon butter**
- 2 **tablespoons parsley, chopped**
- 4 **cups hot cooked rice**
- 3 **sprigs mint**

Preparation

Cut the young, tender steaks into one-inch pieces. Pound lightly and season with salt, pepper, marjoram and thyme. Fry in butter until brown, keeping fire low so meat does not toughen. Remove to a heated platter.

Add the jelly to pan and melt with the meat juices.

Mix the rice with the tablespoon of butter and chopped parsley, fluffing it lightly with a fork. Place the rice in the centre of a heated platter. Arrange the lamb around the rice and pour sauce over meat. Garnish with sprigs of fresh mint.

Jeanette MacDonald

Côte d'Agneau Napolitain

Ingredients to serve 4
2–3 pounds loin of lamb
3 tablespoons vegetable oil
3 small courgettes
1 small aubergine
1 teaspoon flour
½ teaspoon tomato purée
2½ ounces red Bordeaux wine salt
½ teaspoon fresh oregano pepper
2½ oz. beef or lamb stock
6 oz. spaghetti
2 tablespoons butter
3 tomatoes
½ teaspoon each, basil and oregano
2 tablespoons each, parsley and Parmesan cheese

Preparation
Have a loin of lamb boned and rolled by the butcher. The weight should be 2–3 pounds after rolling. Brown in vegetable oil. Remove and keep warm. Skin and chop aubergines into half-inch pieces. Skin courgettes and slice. Brown vegetables in fat from the lamb.

Remove vegetables. Add a teaspoon of flour to fat, adding some butter if the fat has evaporated or been soaked into vegetables. Brown and add tomato purée, red Bordeaux; and reduce by one-quarter.

Season with oregano and fresh pepper and add the stock. Replace meat and vegetables and bake, covered, in a moderate oven (350°F, Mark 4) for 45 minutes.

Boil 6 oz. spaghetti and drain. Melt butter and add the tomatoes, pre-blanched and cut in quarters. Stir gently for 5 minutes. Mix tomatoes into spaghetti. Strain juice from meat and pour over lamb in serving dish. Surround meat with spaghetti. Sprinkle meat with parsley, and spaghetti with freshly grated cheese.

Mrs. Williams

Cold Curried Lamb

Ingredients to serve 4
3–4 pounds leg of lamb
4 oz. butter
1 teaspoon salt
1½ teaspoon marjoram
1 tablespoon flour
2 tablespoons curry powder
1 medium sized onion
1 tart apple
2 cloves garlic
1 tablespoon tomato purée
1 tablespoon chutney
2–3 cups beef stock or lamb stock made from leg of lamb
½ teaspoon thyme
1 tablespoon parsley
2 bay leaves
2 cups boiled rice

Preparation

Have the butcher bone the leg of lamb. Keep the bone for making the stock, if preferred. Cut the meat into pieces about the size of a walnut. Heat 4 oz. of butter in a stew pan until bubbling. Add the lamb with marjoram and salt. Turn frequently. Remove from heat when brown on all sides. Stir flour and curry powder into pan fat.

Chop apple; finely chop onion and add together with the apple to the pan. Crush two cloves of garlic and blend in to curry mixture with tomato purée, chutney, and stock. Add the bouquet garni of bay leaves and parsley. Simmer for about 45 minutes to 1 hour. Remove bouquet garni. Adjust seasoning if necessary. Allow curry to cool. Serve with hot boiled rice.

The Cavalry Club

Curried Hot-Pot

Ingredients
1 tablespoon olive oil
8 mutton cutlets
3 sheep's kidneys
2 onions
1 dozen oysters,
  reserving liquid
3 potatoes, sliced
1 teaspoon salt
  pepper
2 teaspoons curry
  powder
8 small potatoes
1 cup brown sauce

Preparation
Trim fat from mutton cutlets. Place a layer of cutlets at the bottom of an oiled deep earthenware stewpan. Chop kidneys. Slice onions, and add to mutton cutlets, first one layer of kidneys, then a layer of sliced onions. Distribute half of the oysters over the onions. Cover with a layer of thinly sliced potatoes. Sprinkle with salt, pepper, and 1 teaspoon of curry powder.

Begin again with mutton cutlets and continue to alternate layers until dish is full. Make a final layer of the small potatoes, leaving them whole. Pour in oyster liquid and $\frac{3}{4}$ of the brown sauce. (Heat remaining brown sauce just before serving and pour over the top layer.) Bake casserole in a moderately hot oven (375°F, Mark 5) for 1–$1\frac{1}{2}$ hours or until the potatoes are browned.

Colonel Sydney Hankey

West Indian Pepper Pot

Ingredients to serve 6
- 4 tablespoons vegetable oil
- 2 pounds pork loin
- 1 chicken
- 1 shallot, minced
- 2 tablespoons butter
- 1 teaspoon salt
- 1 teaspoon mustard
- dash cayenne pepper
- 1 tablespoon brown sugar
- 2 tablespoons tomato purée
- 1 green pepper
- 1 pound mushrooms
- $\frac{3}{4}$ pint chicken stock
- 1–2 egg yolks

Preparation

Cut pork into pieces the size of a walnut (noisettes). Cut chicken into small serving pieces. Saute pork and chicken in oil until brown on outside. In an earthenware casserole, saute minced shallot for 3 minutes in butter.

Add mustard, dash of cayenne, and salt. Stir in brown sugar, tomato purée and the green pepper cut in thin Juliennes. Slice mushrooms if large, or leave whole if button-size and add with pork and chicken to casserole. Cover with chicken stock. Simmer over medium heat for 45 minutes.

Transfer half a cup of liquid to a clean saucepan. Add one egg yolk, very gradually, stirring to keep the egg from cooking.

As sauce thickens, add more liquid from pan, and the second egg yolk if sauce is not thick enough. Simmer and pour over meat and vegetables in casserole. Serve immediately.

W. Allen,
Chef to Lord Fairhaven

L'Escaloppine de Veau Brownie

Ingredients to serve 2
**2 pounds loin of veal,
juice of half a lemon**
2 tablespoons butter
4 tomatoes
**½ pound fresh
mushrooms**
1 tablespoon parsley
**¼ pint cream
salt
white pepper**
½ cup brandy

Preparation
Trim veal of all fat and gristle. Sprinkle with lemon juice. Pound lightly and leave for half an hour. Make into small flat scallops. Blanch tomatoes and remove skin. Small tomatoes are best for this dish.

In a chafing dish at the table, heat the butter. Saute scallops in butter for 5 minutes. Add the tomatoes, button mushrooms, chopped parsley, and lastly, the cream. Season with salt and white pepper. When dish is heated to the point that the cream is nicely coating the scallops, warm the brandy in a separate enamelled warmer. Pour a half cup of warm brandy over scallops and light, spooning the brandy over the cutlets.

B. Maccagno,
Chef of Luigi's, London

Veal Escalope Coronation

Ingredients to serve 6
 - **2 oz. butter**
 - **4 oz. sliced fresh mushrooms**
 - **12 small veal scallops**
 - **2 tablespoons flour**
 - **$\frac{1}{4}$ cup brandy**
 - **4 oz. tomatoes**
 - **$\frac{1}{4}$ pint single cream**
 - **chopped parsley**
 - **salt**
 - **pepper**

Preparation

Heat the butter in a shallow saute pan until a nutty brown. Add the mushrooms and fry over medium heat. Season the scallops with salt and pepper. Coat very lightly with flour. Add to the mushrooms in pan after mushrooms have cooked about 3 minutes. Turn scallops and fry on other side until golden brown and nearly cooked, about 15 minutes.

Warm brandy in enamelled warmer. Take out one tablespoon of brandy with metal spoon; light and then pour over rest of the brandy, setting it all aflame. While flaming, add to the scallops in the pan.

When flame dies down slightly, add tomatoes to pan and mix well. Stir in cream to make a light sauce. Heat through, never allowing the sauce to boil.

Sprinkle with chopped parsley just before serving.

Chef Losano,
Nurses Home Kitchen, London Hospital

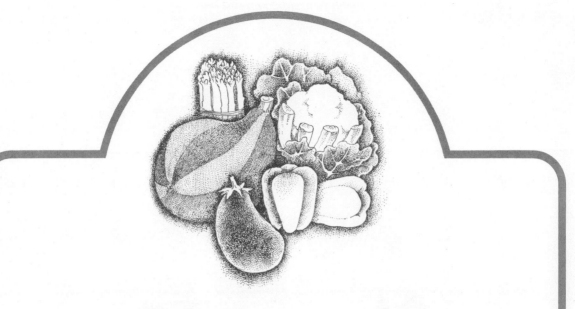

Vegetables

Chef's Salad Mrs. Steel
Luncheon Salad Joan Crawford
Baked Stuffed Artichokes Warner Baxter
Fried Aubergines Their Majesties
King George VI and Queen Elizabeth
L'Aubergine du Cabanon Dissard Claridge's, London
Mushroom Marinade Miss Esme Main,
Cambridgeshire College of Arts and Technology
Flan d'Épinards H.R.H. Princess Alice, Countess of Athlone
Soufflé aux Épinards Their Majesties
King George VI and Queen Elizabeth
Tomatoes au Jour The Marchioness of Cambridge

Chef's Salad

Ingredients tò serve 4
- $\frac{1}{2}$ **pound tongue**
- $\frac{1}{2}$ **pound ham**
- $\frac{1}{2}$ **pound cooked breast of chicken**
- $\frac{1}{4}$ **pound each of Cheddar, Edam and Cheshire cheese**
- **6 hard boiled eggs**
- **6 large tomatoes**
- **1 bunch radishes**
- **1 bunch spring onions**
- **1 large Spanish onion**
- **1 large cos lettuce**
- **1 small cauliflower**
- **1 green pepper**
- **6 black olives**
- **2 tins anchovies**

Preparation

Cut the tongue and ham into strips. Slice the chicken into Julienne strips. Dice the cheese in $\frac{1}{4}$ inch pieces. Chop eggs in eighths or in thick slices, as desired. Quarter the tomatoes and then quarter again. Dice the radishes rather fine.

Chop the onions finely and, if preferred, the Spanish onion can be cut in slices, then separated into rings. Break the cauliflower into individual flowerets. Tear the lettuce with the fingers into generous sized pieces. Place all the ingredients in a large salad bowl. Add the anchovies, chopped, and toss the entire mixture well.

Cut the green pepper into rings and the black olives into rings, if they are pitted, or dice if they are not. Sprinkle the olives among the pepper rings which are laid on top of the salad in a wheel formation.

Chill at least half an hour before serving. Serve a French dressing with a touch of garlic powder, or a creamy Green Goddess dressing apart. This salad makes an excellent entree with jacket potatoes as a complement.

Mrs. Steel

Luncheon Salad

Ingredients to serve 4
4 large tomatoes
½ pint cottage cheese
  fresh chives
  homemade
    mayonnaise
  sour cream
  watercress
  black olives

Preparation
Boil ½ pint water in a large saucepan.
With a slotted spoon, gently put the
tomatoes in to blanch for about 15
seconds, being careful not to crowd
them. Lift out and peel immediately.
Allow to cool.

Cut a fairly large hole in the stem end
of the tomatoes with a very sharp paring
knife. With a small spoon, scoop out the
pips, leaving some of the tomato flesh
and pips at the very bottom.

Combine the cottage cheese with the
chives which have been chopped very
fine. Add a small quantity of home-made
mayonnaise (see recipe, page 122) which
has been mixed with a small amount of
sour cream. The proportion should be
about five to one. Scoop the cottage
cheese into the tomatoes, mounding
slightly on the top.

Chill on a bed of watercress and garnish with black olive rings.

Joan Crawford

Baked Stuffed Artichokes

Ingredients to serve 4
4 large artichokes
½ cup seasoned breadcrumbs
1 tablespoon chopped parsley
2 tablespoons onions
½ cup grated Cheddar cheese
2 tablespoons butter
1 tablespoon olive oil
1 teaspoon minced garlic
4 strips bacon

Preparation

Select large artichokes which are tightly closed at the top and not brown on the outside leaves. Cut off the stem end with a sharp knife. With kitchen scissors cut the tops off the artichokes. Remove the outer leaves, one layer deep.

Spread the remaining leaves apart and fill with the following stuffing: Combine the breadcrumbs with the chopped parsley. Mix in the onions; the spring onion variety is better than ordinary onions, or use shallots. Mix in the grated cheese. Melt the butter and add to the stuffing with olive oil. Dice the garlic very fine and blend thoroughly with the rest of the stuffing.

Bake the artichokes in a large covered pan (375°F, Mark 5) with ½ inch water or broth to keep the bottoms from browning. Set the artichokes upright in the pan propped against each other. Allow 45 minutes to 1½ hours depending upon the size of the artichokes. Garnish each with a strip of crisp bacon.

Warner Baxter

Fried Aubergines

Ingredients to serve 4
2 **aubergines**
salt
1 **pint water**
4 **tablespoons plain**
flour
2 **eggs**
$\frac{2}{3}$ **pint milk**
pinch of sugar
salt
pepper
pinch baking powder
4 **tablespoons**
vegetable oil
4 **tablespoons olive oil**

Preparation
Cut the aubergines in very thin slices.
Place in a shallow, wide dish and cover
with water mixed with $\frac{1}{2}$ teaspoon salt.
Allow to soak for 15 minutes. Dry and
gently squeeze each slice, releasing as
much moisture as possible.

In a large bowl, whisk the eggs. Add
tablespoons flour. Gradually add the
milk just until the batter has reached
medium thickness. Add a pinch of sugar,
the salt and pepper and baking powder.
Mix in the vegetable oil. Set to one side
for about 20 minutes.

Stir the batter a few times, after it has
been allowed to set, to blend the oil once
again. Heat the olive oil in a large frying
pan and fry the aubergine slices which
have been dipped into the batter. Each
slice should be well coated so that the
aubergines will brown evenly and crisp.

**Their Majesties King George VI
and Queen Elizabeth**

L'Aubergine du Cabanon Dissard

Ingredients to serve 4
- **1 onion**
- **4 tomatoes**
- **2 small aubergines**
- **2 small vegetable marrows**
- **1 clove garlic, crushed**
- **$\frac{1}{4}$ cup green pimientoes, or red if green variety unavailable**
- **2–3 tablespoons olive oil**
- **salt**
- **freshly ground pepper**
- **2 tablespoons Parmesan cheese**
- **1 tablespoon breadcrumbs**

Preparation

Chop the onions into small dice. Dip the tomatoes into boiling water to blanch; remove pips, skin and sieve the flesh. Pare the aubergines and the young marrows and cut into thin slices. Chop the pimientoes; finely mince the clove of garlic.

Heat the olive oil and cook the vegetables lightly in oil, one vegetable at a time. After browning, mix the vegetables together, add the crushed garlic and season with salt and freshly ground pepper. Continue cooking in an earthenware au gratin dish tor 12 minutes in a slow oven (325°F, Mark 4). A few minutes before serving, dust lightly with the grated Parmesan cheese mixed with the breadcrumbs, and glaze under the grill.

It is important to cook the dish gently. The vegetables have enough moisture to keep the dish from getting too brown, or sticking. Serve either hot or cold.

Claridge's, London

Mushroom Marinade

Ingredients
1 pound mushrooms
6 tablespoons
vegetable oil
4 tablespoons
tarragon vinegar
1 teaspoon salt
freshly ground black
pepper
2 small cloves garlic
4 sprigs fresh
rosemary
1 teaspoon coriander
seeds
2 tablespoons tomato
purée

Preparation
Select small mushrooms, which are quite firm. Wash and dry well. Slice through the cap and stem and set aside. Combine the oil and vinegar. To this mixture, add the spices and herbs. If fresh rosemary is not available, use the dried variety. Powdered coriander may be substituted for the seeds, but the quantity should be reduced by half.

Marinate the mushrooms in the marinade for about two hours. Transfer to a small flat ovenproof dish. Bake in a slow oven (325°F, Mark 4) for 20 minutes. Serve hot as an accompaniment to eggs or veal. Or allow to cool completely and serve as a condiment. Decorate with snipped parsley.

Miss Esme Main

Flan d'Épinards

Ingredients to serve 4
1 pound spinach
1 medium sized onion
2 teaspoons butter
  salt
  pepper
$\frac{1}{4}$ teaspoon nutmeg
3 egg yolks
$\frac{1}{2}$ pint milk
2 tablespoons cream
$\frac{1}{2}$ cup cream

Preparation
Prepare flan case and bake according to recipe for Provence Flan (see page 12). Wash spinach leaves. Do not dry. Put the spinach in a medium saucepan with just the moisture on the leaves from washing. Add a small pat of butter and steam, covered, over low heat for about 5 minutes. Chop fine. Chop the onion into dice and fry in butter for a few minutes before adding spinach. Season to taste with salt, pepper and nutmeg.

Heat through, and spoon into the prepared flan case. Flatten out the mixture to about a quarter of an inch depth and spread flat with a broad palette or spatula knife. Make a raw cheese custard by combining the three egg yolks with $\frac{1}{2}$ pint milk and the cream. Mix in two-thirds of the cheese. Pour custard over the spinach in flan case. Scatter the remaining cheese over the top and bake in a moderate oven (350°F, Mark 4) for about 40 minutes or until the custard is set and browned. Cut in quarters.

H.R.H. Princess Alice,
Countess of Athlone

Soufflé aux Épinards

Ingredients to serve 4
6 eggs
6 large tablespoons
  cream
3 tablespoons grated
  Parmesan cheese
3 tablespoons purée
  of spinach
  salt, pepper
  cayenne pepper
1 teaspoon grated
  cheese

Preparation
Separate the yolks and whites of the eggs, putting the whites in a copper bowl, ready for beating.

Put the yolks in a medium-sized saute pan and add the cream and grated cheese. Mix well and cook slowly over medium heat, stirring all the time, until the mixture thickens. The mixture must be heated through, but never come to the boiling point. Put the spinach through a sieve until it is of a properly puréed consistency. Add to the egg mixture and heat through. Season with salt, pepper and cayenne.

Whisk the egg whites until they stand in stiff peaks. Fold in $\frac{1}{3}$ of the stiffly beaten whites to lighten the spinach and egg mixture. Fold in well with a spatula using a cutting motion. Add the remaining egg whites, mixing just enough to blend them in lightly.

Butter a soufflé case well and sprinkle with 1 teaspoon of grated Parmesan cheese. Fill up to the level of the top of the case. Make a band of greased brown paper around the top edge and fasten, making a collar. Sprinkle with Parmesan cheese and bake in a hot oven (375°F, Mark 5) for 25–35 minutes, depending on the evenness of temperature.

Their Majesties King George VI
and Queen Elizabeth

Tomatoes au Jour

Ingredients
olive oil
1½ pounds tomatoes
1 tablespoon chopped parsley
1 clove garlic
2 oz. breadcrumbs or cooked small macaroni shells
2–3 oz. grated Parmesan cheese
salt
pepper

Preparation
Stem the tomatoes and wipe with a piece of kitchen towelling moistened in olive oil. Cut the tomatoes in two. Cover the bottom of a greased shallow fireproof dish with half the tomatoes, skin side down. Season.

Pour a tablespoon of olive oil over the tops and sprinkle with chopped parsley. Cover with the breadcrumbs or macaroni. If using macaroni, season with salt and pepper and coat lightly with a small pat of butter while still warm.

On each breadcrumb layer, place the remaining tomato halves, making a whole tomato. Season and sprinkle with olive oil. Dust Parmesan cheese over the tops and cook in a slow oven (325°F, Mark 3) for about 40 minutes.

The Marchioness of Cambridge

Sauces and Preserves

Mayonnaise H.M. Queen Elizabeth, The Queen Mother
Cumberland Sauce Mrs. Chell, Cook to the Countess Roberts
Sauce Venaison à la Créme H.R.H. Princess Alice,
Countess of Athlone
Half-Hour Rapsberry Jam Mrs. Vickers
Orange Marmalade Mrs. Laurence Carr

Mayonnaise

Ingredients

3 fresh egg yolks
salt to taste
$\frac{1}{4}$–1 **teaspoon mustard**
1 **pint vegetable oil**
$\frac{1}{4}$ **pint tarragon**
vinegar

Preparation

Beat the egg yolks with the salt and mustard until thick, and a lemon colour. If the yolks are at room temperature, and beaten to the proper point, they will be much better able to absorb the oil, and make the proper emulsion.

Alternately whisk in the oil and the vinegar by droplets, very gradually, until the emulsion process begins. It is very important to continue beating the sauce while adding the droplets of oil and vinegar.

If using the mixer or blender, mix on high speed, being sure that all ingredients are well blended to achieve a thick substance. Add a little hot vinegar as the final step. The consistency should be a creamy but firm mixture.

H.M. Queen Elizabeth,
The Queen Mother

122

Cumberland Sauce

Ingredients
**4 tablespoons red
  currant jelly**
$\frac{1}{3}$ cup port
**1 teaspoon shallots
  rind of half an
    orange**
**1 teaspoon mustard
  juice of one orange
  juice of half a lemon
  dash cayenne pepper
  dash powdered
    ginger**

Preparation
Place the red currant jelly in a saucepan over boiling water. Stir, until the jelly is soft. Add the port and shallots which have been chopped very fine.

With a small sharp knife, cut the orange rind into Julienne strips. Add to the sauce. Stir in mustard and the juice of one orange and half a lemon. Add a dash of cayenne pepper and an equal amount of powdered ginger. Blend all ingredients together and allow to rest for a few hours to blend all ingredients.

This sauce makes an excellent accompaniment for braised tongue, cold beef, or baked ham.

Mrs. Chell,
Cook to the Countess Roberts

Sauce Venaison à la Crème

Ingredients
- **1 onion**
- **1 carrot**
- **small bunch parsley**
- **sprig of fresh thyme**
- **1 bay leaf**
- **1 clove**
- **12 peppercorns**
- **1 oz. butter**
- **1 lb. venison bones and trimmings**
- **2 oz. wine vinegar**
- **2 oz. port**
- **$\frac{1}{2}$ pint brown sauce**
- **$\frac{1}{2}$ pint stock**
- **$\frac{1}{2}$ pint cream**
- **salt**

Brown sauce:
- **2 tablespoons butter**
- **2 medium carrots, diced**
- **1 onion, chopped**
- **2 sprigs parsley**
- **pinch thyme**
- **bay leaf**
- **2 tablespoons flour**
- **1 cup dry white wine**
- **$1\frac{1}{2}$ cup consomme**
- **1 tablespoon tomato paste**
- **$\frac{1}{2}$ teaspoon salt**
- **$\frac{1}{4}$ teaspoon pepper**

Preparation
Skin the onion; peel carrot and cut both vegetables in thin slices. Fry together with parsley, thyme, bay leaf, clove and peppercorns in 1 oz. butter.

Add one pound of bones and trimmings of venison. Blend in the vinegar, which can be wine vinegar for a distinctive flavour, or cider vinegar. Add the port and simmer until the liquid is reduced by half.

Stir in the $\frac{1}{2}$ pint of stock and $\frac{1}{2}$ pint of brown sauce made by the following method: Melt the butter; add the vegetables and seasonings. Cook over low heat until the vegetables brown. Stir in flour and cook until slightly brown. Add the wine and the consomme; stir in tomato paste, salt and pepper. Bring to a boil and simmer 20 minutes. Strain.

Pour the venison sauce into a clean saucepan and add the cream. Reduce the sauce until it is of desired consistency. Correct seasoning if necessary.

**H.R.H. Princess Alice,
Countess of Athlone**

Half-Hour Raspberry Jam

Ingredients
Proportions are 1 pound of fruit to 1 pound of sugar

Preparation
Place the fruit in the preserving pan. Heat gently at first until the juice begins to flow. Then bring to a boil and allow to boil quickly for 5 minutes.

Add the sugar, stirring gently with a broad wooden spoon. Bring the jam to a boil again, and allow to boil for 5 to 7 minutes. Do not overcook. If the sugar is warmed slightly before adding to the fruit, it will dissolve more rapidly.

Pour the jam into a jug so the process of pouring into the jars is easier. Cover the jars immediately with a round of waxed paper, making sure the disc touches the whole surface of the jam. A cover of plastic wrap, wiped with a damp cloth will ensure a good seal. This recipe is only suitable for raspberry jam.

Mrs. Vickers

Orange Marmalade

Ingredients
**10 pounds Seville
   oranges**
 **6 pounds sweet
   oranges**
12 pounds loaf sugar
 6 pints cold water

Preparation
Cut the oranges in half and take off the skins without tearing them, using the handle of a spoon. Boil the skins until tender, between $1\frac{1}{2}$ and 2 hours. Plunge the skins into cold water to remove the bitterness.

Drain on a sieve and scrape off as much of the soft white pith as possible. Cut the skins into fine Julienne strips.

Heat the sugar with the water to clarify. Let the sugar and water mixture boil for 5 minutes. Remgve the pips from the centre of the oranges. Add the orange pulp and the Julienne strips of peel to the sugar and boil slowly for 1 hour.

If the marmalade is cooled slightly, the shreds of rind will remain distributed evenly throughout the jam.

Mrs. Laurence Carr

Desserts

Crème Brulée Their Majesties King George VI and Queen Elizabeth
Custard Tarts Sonja Henie
Cerises Flambées The Marchioness of Cambridge
Winter Dessert Gloria Stuart
Meringues Café Mrs. Fraser, Cook to Philip Hodgson, Esq.
Le Cussy or Progrès Monsieur Avignon, Chef of the Ritz
Hotel, London
Crêpes St. James Gerald Boxiosi, Boodle's, London
Syrup Tart Chef to the Roehampton Club
Zwetschken Knödeln The Lady Louis Mountbatten
Petits Babas H.R.H. Princess Alice, Countess of Athlone
Medenham Cake The Hon. Mrs. Sturdy
Chantilly Deep Apple Pie Nelson Eddy
Ruby Pie Victor McLaghlan
Pouding Florida H.R.H. The Duchess of Gloucester
Sago Plum Pudding Miss Lynch

Crème Brulée

Ingredients to serve 4
½ **pint cream**
3 yolks of eggs
1 tablespoon sugar
  vanilla
2 teaspoons icing
  sugar

Preparation
This custard is cooked very slowly in the oven like a crème caramel. In a medium-sized bowl, add egg yolks, one at a time to the cream. Mix in the castor sugar and a dash of vanilla. Mix thoroughly but do not let mixture become frothy. Pour into individual custard cups or dariole moulds.

Cook in slow oven (325°F, Mark 3) for 45 minutes. When the custard is firmly set, sprinkle tops with icing sugar. Glaze under grill, being careful that the tops are not too brown. Chill for several hours.

**Their Majesties King George VI
and Queen Elizabeth**

Custard Tarts

Ingredients to serve 4

- 4 **egg yolks**
- 2 **teaspoons plain flour**
- 2 **tablespoons castor sugar**
- $\frac{3}{4}$ **cup cream**
- 1 **teaspoon vanilla**
- $2\frac{1}{8}$ **cup flour**
- $\frac{1}{3}$ **pound butter**
- 3 **tablespoons castor sugar**

Preparation

Combine two of the egg yolks, flour and sugar in a double boiler. Combine milk and cream. Beat the egg and flour mixture over medium heat for two minutes. Gradually add milk and cream mixture. Cook until thick and smooth. Remove from heat and continue to beat until partially cooled. Add one teaspoon vanilla.

Combine quickly two and one-eighths cup flour with the remaining two egg yolks, butter and three tablespoons sugar. Line small fluted tins with this mixture and bake "blind" in hot oven (450°F, Mark 8) for about 5 minutes.

Fill cases with custard mixture. Set on a baking sheet and bake in oven (375°F, Mark 5) for 15 minutes or until set. Allow to cool betore serving.

Sonja Henie

Cerises Flambées

Ingredients to serve 4
**1 tin pitted black
cherries
$\frac{1}{2}$ teaspoon cornflour
$\frac{1}{4}$ cup Kirsch
1 pint vanilla ice
cream**

Preparation
Strain juice from the black cherries into
a saucepan. Set fruit aside. Bring the
juice to a boil, about 4 minutes over
medium high heat. Thicken with cornflour. When the syrup coats a wooden
spoon it is cooked through.

Transfer cherries to a soufflé dish.
Pour syrup over fruit. Heat the Kirsch
in an enamelled warming pot. Heat a
large metal spoon and dip into the heated
Kirsch. Light the liqueur in the spoon
and pour over the cherries just before
serving, adding the rest of the heated
Kirsch at the last minute. Serve over
vanilla ice cream.

The Marchioness of Cambridge

Winter Dessert

Ingredients to serve 6
4 eggs
½ cup brown sugar
½ cup honey
2 cups milk
1 cup cream
¼ teaspoon salt
   dash nutmeg
6 tart apples
   small piece beef suet
1 pint double cream
1 teaspoon rum
   flavouring

Preparation

Prepare custard: beat eggs until frothy. Gradually beat in first the brown sugar, then the honey. Combine milk and cream. Add to the egg and sugar mixture, together with the salt. Sprinkle nutmeg over the surface.

Peel apples, cut in half and remove cores with a sharp knife. Place cut half downward in a flat baking dish and cover with custard.

Take a firm piece of beef suet and chop finely until it makes about two tablespoons. Sprinkle over the top of the custard and apples and bake in a moderate oven (350°F, Mark 4) until the apples are tender when pierced with a fork, about 20 minutes.

Whip cream until firm, beating in a teaspoon of rum flavouring after about 3 minutes of mixing. Serve with custard apples.

Gloria Stuart

Meringues Café

Ingredients to make
meringues
4 whites of eggs
4 oz. castor sugar
4 oz. chopped walnuts
  coffee essence
    sufficient to colour
    and flavour
1 pint whipped cream
1 teaspoon shortening
1 teaspoon flour

Preparation
Whip the eggs stiffly. Add the sugar gradually to the whites. Then fold in the walnuts and the coffee essence. Add just enough to colour.

Grease a baking sheet with shortening and dust with flour. Put mixture onto the prepared tin in six portions.

Bake in a slow oven (200°F, Mark 1/4) for 2–3 hours or until dry and crisp. When the meringues are cold, spread five of them with coffee-flavoured whipped cream. Pile in a dish with the plain one on top. Cover the top and sides with unflavoured whipped cream.

Alternatively, to make chantilly meringues, double the above recipe, omitting the coffee essence. Sandwich the baked meringues in pairs with a mixture of $\frac{1}{4}$ pint double cream, sweetened with 2 teaspoons sugar and drop of vanilla essence, whipped and piped in between each sandwich. Decorate with citron and glacé cherries in flower formations.

Mrs. Fraser,
Cook to Philip Hodgson, Esq.

Le Cussy or Progrès

Ingredients to serve 4
The whites of 8 eggs, well whipped
$\frac{1}{4}$ **pound ground hazel nuts**
$\frac{1}{2}$ **pound ground almonds**
$\frac{3}{4}$ **pound castor sugar**
1 teaspoon each, flour and butter
$\frac{2}{3}$ **cup chopped almonds**
$\frac{1}{2}$ **cup pastry cream**
$\frac{1}{2}$ **cup buttered cream**

Preparation

Mix the egg whites, ground nuts and sugar together. Press mixture through a piping bag. Form it into a round shape, rope fashion on a tray which has been buttered and floured. Bake in a low oven (300°F, Mark 2) for 20–30 minutes or until done.

Cut the cake into halves. Sprinkle one half with chopped almonds. Prepare a pastry cream (see Crêpes St. James recipe, page 134) with Kirsch instead of brandy. Add the buttered cream and blend. Cover both halves of the cake with the cream mixture and place the half with the chopped almonds on top.

It is the usual practice to prepare this cake a day beforehand to allow it to become a bit soft.

Monsieur Avignon,
Chef of the Ritz Hotel, London

Crêpes St. James

Ingredients to serve 5
Pancakes:
- **1 pint milk**
- **3 oz. flour**
- **2 eggs**
  cream (optional)

Pastry cream:
- **8 oz. sugar**
- **1 pint milk**
- **6 egg yolks**
- **2 oz. flour**
- **1 tablespoon brandy**
- **½ cup brandy**
  flavoured with
  2 teaspoons honey
- **1 tablespoon unsalted**
  butter

Preparation

Combine ingredients for pancakes. Allow mixture to stand for at least one hour. Cook pancakes in a crêpe pan by spooning a small ladle full of batter into pan and swirling liquid to coat entire bottom of pan. Cook only a few minutes on each side. Longer cooking will toughen the pancake. Grease and sugar some grease-proof paper and lay cooked pancakes on layers of the paper, so they rest separately.

To make pastry cream, boil milk. Beat eggs and sugar together. When well mixed, incorporate flour in the egg and sugar mixture. Add the boiling milk and return mixture to heat. Stir until it comes to a boil again. Flavour with brandy.

Spoon pastry cream into the middle of each pancake and roll up. Warm butter in copper serving dish; add pancakes and cook gently for one minute. Spoon honeyed brandy over each pancake. At last moment, add a few drops of brandy, and flame.

Part of the menu which won first prize in the Mouton Cadet 1972 Competition.

Gerald Boxiosi,
Boodle's, London

Syrup Tart

Ingredients to serve 4
Shortcrust pastry:
8 oz. plain flour
4 oz. butter or
  margarine
$\frac{1}{8}$ pound sugar
1 egg
Filling:
6 tablespoons golden
  syrup
6 tablespoons
  breadcrumbs

Preparation
Make shortcrust pastry in the usual manner, using the above proportions. If desired, the crust can be baked "blind" for a few minutes so the filling does not have a chance to soak into the crust.

Line a pie plate or floured ring with the pastry and bake a few minutes or fill directly with syrup and crumbs mixed together. Bake in hot oven (425°F, Mark 7) for 20–30 minutes. Remove from plate and transfer to a dish. Serve hot with ice cream if desired, or pass double cream with it.

If preferred, extra shortcrust pastry may be made to decorate the top with a latticework overcrust, and then baked.

The Chef of the Roehampton Club

Zwetschken Knödeln

Ingredients to serve 6

6 oz. flour
  pinch salt
4 potatoes, baked
1 tablespoon cream
1 egg yolk
1 whole egg
3 pounds small plums
  lump sugar
1 cup breadcrumbs
4 oz. butter
½ cup sugar, flavoured
  with vanilla pod

Preparation

Rub the baked potatoes through a sieve or ricer. In a bowl, combine flour, a pinch of salt, and the sieved potatoes. Blend in the egg yolk and the whole egg. Mix quickly to a stiff paste.

Remove the stones from the plums. Insert in each plum a lump of sugar. Cover each plum well with the paste so that no opening can be seen. Drop each into simmering water with a slotted spoon. Simmer the dumplings for 10 minutes; drain on a sieve or kitchen towelling.

Saute the breadcrumbs to a golden colour in butter. Add the vanilla-flavoured sugar. Sprinkle over plum dumplings. Serve very hot. Small apricots can be used instead of plums.

The Lady Louis Mountbatten

Petits Babas

Ingredients to serve 6
½ **pound flour**
½ **oz. yeast**
¼ **pound butter**
5 eggs
1 oz. sugar
½ **teaspoon salt**
Syrup:
4 tablespoons honey
4 tablespoons water
1 teaspoon rum
½ **cup Mirabelle**
 cherries
1 teaspoon Kirsch

Preparation
Mix yeast with sugar and a little flour; add ¼ cup tepid water. Place the remainder of the flour in a basin, making a well in the centre and pour in the yeast mixture. Allow to stand in a warm place for 25 minutes, until yeast is proved.

Melt butter and stir into mixture with the salt. Beat eggs and add to flour mixture; work well. Place in greased dariole moulds and cover with sheet of lightly greased paper. Allow to rise until moulds are ⅔ full. Bake in moderate hot oven (375°F, Mark 5) for 20 minutes.

Make syrup by combining honey with water in a saucepan. Add rum and heat until slightly thickened. When babas are cool, soak in hot syrup. Heat the Kirsch in a metal spoon over flame. Light and pour over cherries. Mound cherries in centre of dish and surround with babas.

**H.R.H. Princess Alice,
Countess of Athlone**

Medenham Cake

Ingredients to serve 6
7 oz. butter
7 oz. plain flour
**2 oz. dark Barbados
sugar**
**2 tablespoons apricot
jam**

Preparation
Mix butter, flour and sugar together. Place on a slab and work until well mixed and a workable dough. Make two bands of paper, $1\frac{1}{2}$ inches deep and join together to make the size of the cake, about 6 inches across.

Take half the mixture and knead out to the size of the paper. Then do the same with the other half. Place in a moderate oven (350°F, Mark 4) on a baking tin for 20 minutes. It should be springy to the touch when done. Do not handle until quite cold.

Spread the bottom layer with apricot jam; put one layer on top of the other and serve.

This cake must be eaten the day it is made.

The Hon. Mrs. Sturdy

Chantilly Deep Apple Pie

Ingredients to serve 6
**5 cups apples, thinly
sliced
$\frac{1}{2}$ cup castor sugar
$\frac{1}{2}$ cup brown sugar,
firmly packed
$\frac{1}{8}$ teaspoon allspice
$\frac{1}{2}$ teaspoon cinnamon
2 tablespoons butter
8 oz. shortcrust pastry
$\frac{1}{4}$ cup milk
$\frac{1}{4}$ cup castor sugar
$\frac{1}{2}$ cup thin cream**

Preparation
Fill an oblong baking dish half full of
sliced apples. Mix the sugars, allspice,
and cinnamon together. Sprinkle half
over the apples, add the remaining
apples and cover with the rest of the
sugar mixture. Dot with butter.

Roll some shortcrust pastry into a
rectangle $\frac{1}{4}$ inch thick and cut five
decorative openings in the centre.

Fit the dough over the apples, turning
under a $\frac{1}{2}$ inch edge. Seal the edges of the
pie. Brush with milk or water and
sprinkle with sugar. Bake in hot oven
(425°F, Mark 7) for 30–40 minutes.
Pour cream into the pie through the
openings about 5 minutes before taking
from the oven. Serve warm cut in squares.

Nelson Eddy

Ruby Pie

Ingredients to serve 6
- 2½ cups cranberries
- 1¾ cups sugar
- 1½ cups cold water
- 4 teaspoons butter
- 6 bananas
- 4 oz. shortcrust pastry

Preparation

Wash cranberries, discarding the soft or spoilt berries. Add 1¾ cups sugar and cover with the water. Cook in a covered saucepan until the berries stop popping.

Put one-third of the berries into a deep well-greased pie tin. Add a layer of the bananas, thinly sliced. Cover with another layer of berries, and continue alternating berries and bananas until all fruit is used.

Cover fruit with the shortcrust pastry rolled out about ¼ inch thick. Be sure the pastry is fitted closely around the edge of the dish. Slash the crust and bake in a hot oven for 15 minutes (425°F, Mark 7). Reduce heat to moderate (350°F, Mark 4) and continue baking for 15 minutes more, or until the crust is well browned.

Victor McLaghlan

Pouding Florida

Ingredients to serve 4
1 teaspoon butter
1 pint milk
1 oz. sugar
2 oz. butter
rind of one lemon, finely chopped
2 oz. French ground rice
3 eggs
½ cup fine breadcrumbs or crushed biscuit crumbs
apricot sauce

Preparation
Butter well a charlotte mould. Sprinkle with either breadcrumbs, browned in butter, or crushed ginger biscuit crumbs.

Place milk, sugar, lemon peel, and butter in a pan and bring to the boil. Add the French ground rice and allow to cool.

Separate eggs; whisk whites until stiff. Stir the yolks of the eggs into the rice mixture. Fold in the stiffly beaten whites. Steam for 1–1½ hours and serve with apricot sauce:

Prepare sauce by pressing one pound of stewed apricots through a sieve. Add enough simple sugar syrup to make a purée. Boil, stirring constantly with a wooden spoon. When sauce coats spoon, take off the fire and cool.

H.R.H. The Duchess of Gloucester

141

Sago Plum Pudding

Ingredients to serve 6
- **4 tablespoons sago**
- **1½ cup milk**
- **½ teaspoon bicarbonate of soda**
- **3 tablespoons butter**
- **½ cup sugar**
- **1 cup raisins**
- **1 cup fine white breadcrumbs**
- **pinch salt**
- **¼–½ teaspoon vanilla**
- **¼ teaspoon almond essence**

Hard sauce:
- **⅓ cup butter**
- **1 cup powdered sugar**
- **½ teaspoon nutmeg**
- **3 tablespoons milk**

Preparation

Soak sago in the 1½ cups milk with the bicarbonate of soda overnight. Cream butter with the sugar until the butter is quite grainy. Add raisins, breadcrumbs, the sago, milk and a pinch of salt. Add vanilla essence and almond essence to taste. Pour into a greased bowl, with deep sides, or pudding mould and steam for 4–4½ hours, covered.

Serve with hard sauce and whipped cream, if preferred. To make hard sauce, cream butter and sugar together. Add nutmeg and beat to a white foam. Add the milk a tablespoon at a time until sauce is of proper consistency.

Miss Lynch

INDEX